Along The Way

By

Carole Hutch

ISBN: 0-7596-6405-6 (e-book)
ISBN: 0-7596-6406-4 (Paperback)
ISBN: 0-7596-6407-2 (Hardcover)

This book is printed on acid free paper.

1stBooks - rev. 01/09/03

CHAPTER ONE

The shedding of tears never softened the blow and now fearing their desperate and inescapable final decision to leave their native land and forsake their many friends may have been an irreversible mistake, but necessary for the trio of troubled and bedraggled travelers who sat quite conspicuously proud in a stiff upright position while clutching tightly to their valises which contained amounts of cash, in essence their past, present and future.

The trio consisted of two men and a woman. The older man, very handsome with curly blonde hair and blue eyes and considered the leader, the serious thinker, named Hans, retrieved a battered and crumpled magazine advertisement and studied it to verify their reason for being on the speeding train South.

Even though the view was frustratingly beautiful with its sameness of never ending trees, interrupted by rolling hills and bright green pastures dotted with cattle and occasionally with houses, barns, and small cities which had many people walking about, the trio didn't seem to notice any of the beauty.

Granting their terrified and defeated parents their deathbed wish for them to seek freedom in America, Hans, his younger sister, Gerta, who was very plain with blue eyes and blonde hair and very bitter over leaving, and his younger brother, Abram, short, stocky and cute, also with blonde hair and blue eyes.

They had successfully exchanged good fertile land, sturdy house, and prized family possessions for money to travel to America to exercise their flight to freedom. Their land had been worked by a member of the Tillers family for many generations and they were hoping to make a new start in America preferably on the land since that profession was all they knew. It was a heavy cross to bear to be the last holders of the Tillers' legacy and to burden themselves with their sense of loss and failure and dejected defeat which were hanging heavily in their hearts and depriving them of any feeling of security or adventure, but hope of a better life was their goal which kept them calm. If their parents wanted them to seek freedom in a new land by urging them to sell unlimited personal treasures, then they would succeed with His help while their parents watched over them. In that belief, they dared.

Getting off the boat in the East Coast harbor had excited them into a false sense of security. Even after finding factory jobs, they knew the intense overcrowding of the big city was not for them. They felt the message in the ad begging for a farm manager down South was manna from heaven and a good omen of what Mama and Papa wanted for them.

Gerta, a victim of habit and assuming her position as being the lady of the house, although a moving house, and responding to her Mama's teachings served the last of their prepared food and was disposing of the remains while the conductor in his blue suit and hat hurriedly made his way through the coach while touching each seat as he began announcing, "Longbranch, the next stop, Longbranch." He tipped his hat to the anxious trio as he went by and spoke, "This is your destination. I wish you luck in your chosen country."

Neither mentioned the fear of being different and not making it in such a strange land because Hans was in charge of their destiny and they had pledged their trust and support in him after promising Mama and Papa they would follow him to ruin or success. Somehow they knew Hans would fulfill their parents' bequest. After all, the leader of their country was a meglomaniac and they were anxious to begin a new life elsewhere, so responding to the many good reports of available work and prosperity for anyone who wanted it, they set out for America.

After realizing the danger of serving a leader who worshipped power and cruelly used his people to realize his dream, they were eager to escape to America. They stretched out tall and thin as they assumed an air of courageous composure to distill their fear that they would never be received with proper status they had possessed before becoming aliens, since they were aware of staring eyes as they basked in the warm sunshine after detraining. They felt relieved as they watched all the passengers being met by caring people.

Someone was coming toward them, evidently their new boss man, a very tall and handsome but rugged and thin man, in faded blue overalls and blue denim shirt with a well-worn straw hat on his head, was there to meet them—the hat was badly stained with sweat and dust. Gerta thought perhaps he certainly needed a new one. His darkly tanned exposed skin was very weather-beaten, vaguely resembling cowhide leather. As he approached them cautiously, his smile was wholesome and genuine as he shook hands. While introductions were made, he was very gracious. He was shocked and surprised at the lack of luggage but neither explained.

Soon they were riding along in a handsome black, shiny car on country roads, making many turns and being charmed by the gracious manner their new boss waved at all the folks along the way.

Entire families, with many happy and noisy children, were walking along on the side of the road and standing still and nodding howdy as the car passed slowly. Others were either riding mules bareback with their harness on or were leading them. Evidently their day's work was done until tomorrow between sunrise and sunset when they toiled.

Everyone, young and old, wore straw hats, apparently to protect themselves from the hot sun, but under the hats could be seen kerchiefs or colorful head bands covering their hair, probably from the dust, or to chase the aggravating tiny insects which gathered in or near their eyes, ears and nose in such a manner they were alarmed. Gerta was terrified at having to fan the attacking insects with her hands without alarming them. She did not even like the word, gnat, and hated the insect intensely enough to return to her native land. She turned her interest toward the many workers.

Their clothes showed obvious sweat stains and through the opened window, she knew they were sweating. Hans, Abram and Gerta rejoiced that their neighbors were hard working people of the land and they hoped to be accepted as friendly neighbors who also enjoyed hard work; however, rewarding by its nature.

Gerta and Abram exchanged smiles of curiosity as Hans and Doyle rambled on about their journey from home and their anticipated new life with the Hepstarts, Doyle and his sister Lutricia. Doyle apologized for his difficulty in understanding their accent but everyone laughed when Hans explained he couldn't understand too much that Doyle was saying in his slow southern drawl.

Lutricia, a charming, shy lady, with soft brown hair, grey eyes and very fair skin, met them at the gate of the white picket fence that surrounded the front of the white frame house. She wasn't as tall as her brother and not as weather-beaten but suffered from her shyness and appeared frail and not strong like Gerta. She stepped forward and greeted them very cordially and smiled sweetly becoming a vision of loveliness as she slowly extended her hand to Hans, then Abram and then Gerta, however, lowering her eyes slowly to the floor as she shook their hands. She recovered and made them feel very welcomed, as she graciously led them to the quite formal and spacious dining room, bidding them to have a seat as she served them iced tea and lady finger cookies. She was the perfect hostess to her guests, total strangers from a strange land and strange clothes.

Sharing chores and pleasures of the large house with Doyle and Lutricia was not an apparent imposition but even with the great amount of acreage, Abram and Gerta realized that only Hans was happy with their new life and after many serious conferences, Abram was dispatched to law school and Gerta to become a librarian.

Due to excessive homesickness, after graduation, the two wayward siblings, not wishing to live apart, (Abram and Gerta) returned to Longbranch and became part of the community and at the end of the waiting period, the three became naturalized citizens with the aid of Mr. Hepstart and Lutricia. They rejoiced at the planned celebration which brought many nearby neighbors whom the trio had not met.

When Abram opened his law practice in Longbranch, he sensed he might starve with the living he was eking from his practice. He developed American know-how and began courting the banker's daughter who was sweet on him. The more he was seen in public with her on his arm, the more his practice grew. He would probably remain a poor lawyer, he feared, without taking a wife.

When he realized he could live on his income and his share of his parents' estate, Abram married the banker's daughter, Merle, and he became a happy

Longbranch native and participated in all its events. Merle and Abram produced one son, Jeremiah, who followed in the footsteps of his father by becoming a lawyer but with a more lucrative practice since he met with no obstacles. They settled permanently in Longbranch and watched their roots grow and expand. Abram served for many years as Mayor and incorporated many political strategies that interested the town.

The spirit of kinship and closeness among Abram, Gerta and Hans remained steadfast, even after Gerta married Edward Green, a confirmed and eccentric bachelor who was her employer as head librarian. It was a very long courtship and many onlookers thought they were too peculiar to wed.

Hans married Lutricia as everyone predicted he would. Hans had been the ambitious sibling. After giving Abram and Gerta their fair share and using his share, he succeeded in buying nearly 9000 acres of good fertile land which he leased to hard working farmers, mostly immigrants like him. He doled out to them and kept their acreage around 350 acres and helped them build comfortable houses on their prescribed acres and always urged them to make many changes by diversifying and not overworking their fertile land.

Hans brought Doyle's farm up to a greater prosperity which caused a secure feeling for Doyle to consider courting and marrying a young lady he had swooned over for years. Doyle and his young wife, Juanita Clarke, were active in their church and community and continued to work hard but enjoyed a genteel and successful social life.

Hans, although independently wealthy, still managed Doyle's farm and built on his land, a small one bedroom cottage for him and Lutricia because his wife, whom he cherished, had a health problem and was advised not to have children if she wished to live to be an old lady.

The enterprising young man, Hans, turned all his profits over to Abram for investing; consequently, he became a wealthy and potentially affluent man but he never left his home to become an active member anyplace. He was unhappy because World War II had devastated him since all the people he had known as a young man were either killed or had disappeared. He never mentioned his pain to anyone but Lutricia, moreover, he regretted he was too old to serve in his new country's fight for freedom since his new country had entered war to guarantee all the citizens their freedom.

He and Lutricia lived a happy idylic life on the farm. Each lived for the other and enjoyed their total interdependence as Gerta and Edward became hard hearted, selfish, very doubting and obviously mean and stayed married only because they were afraid of losing their jobs and prestige in the city if they divorced. Hans was concerned for his sister so he had a house built for them to add to their joy, and nothing helped.

Doyle and Juanita were killed in an automobile accident while on their vacation to the coast. Hans handled everything and found Doyle had left his entire estate to Lutricia so he asked Abram to settle the affair since Juanita had no relatives.

Hans considered moving back in the old home but Lutricia preferred the coziness of her honeymoon cottage so Hans again sought new families to lease the same small acreage as he was using successfully with his estate. There was a big house and barn raising as the new tenants signed their leases and moved onto their land, working it by day and sleeping in various barns and sheds of generous neighbors by night until their homes were available. The area was developing into a large community but everyone seemed delighted to work with Abram and Hans who surprised them with their dedicated generosity, by sharing their land resources and apparently void of greed.

After many years of marriage, Lutricia became pregnant and defied doctor's request for abortion since they considered it His plan. Hans, over the dire prediction, did everything for her. He added a large nursery to their cottage and together they bought all that a baby needed and delighted in their efforts. He showered her with love and devotion. He engaged a midwife, Emily Jackson, in case the doctor was delayed in arriving at the farm because he wanted his child to be born at home and for his wife to die there if that was what it would be. He loved his home where everything was shared, therefore, they would share in birth and death also if necessary.

Dr. Lane informed them of the danger but Hans and Lutricia were adamant so the midwife was briefed by Dr. Lane on what to do in his absence to guarantee her and the baby making it, since he was hoping for a miracle, because he knew one was definitely needed.

Poor Lutricia was in her tenth hour of labor when Dr. Lane arrived to find Emily carrying out his orders. Hans never left her and was at her bedside when Sophee was born and as he held her, he wept for relief and joy at the beautiful blonde creature he and his loving wife had produced, and without the loss of Lutricia. He placed their baby in his wife's arms and together they gave thanks for such a precious gift and together named her Sophee, their chosen name. They dared to rejoice as they continued to share their love and their child, to them a miracle.

Before sundown of the following day, their happiness was shattered as Hans noticed Lutricia's weakening condition and remaining true to his practical and logical ways, drove in to Longbranch to prepare a will, leaving his newborn the entire bulk of his estate, guaranteeing the land and all his possessions to be handed down without ever being sold as long as there was an heir and if no heir, to his landowners free and clear. He appointed Abram executor and stipulated that in the event of his and Lutricia's death, Gerta and Edward were to be Sophee's guardians since they had no children, even though Hans never asked if they wanted his and Lutricia's child. Family took care of family.

Abram responded to Hans' request and recorded his will without questions since he had always trusted and admired his older brother, even though he sensed gloom and despair but Abram was not one to pry. However, Abram became troubled by the request to bury Hans and his wife under the old cedar tree on his farm.

On the fifth day after her child's birth, Lutricia died quietly in her husband's arms. Hans, distraught with grief but forcefully composed himself and asked Emily quietly to take the baby and her entire nursery to Gerta and to leave at that very minute and he begged her to remain with Sophee until she didn't need her. He helped Emily load the truck, held Sophee tightly, kissed her goodbye, asked her forgiveness. He placed the baby gently in Emily's arms, turned and walked toward the cottage and raised his hand in farewell.

Emily obeyed his every direction as she had promised by waiting to call the undertaker, Dr. Lane and the sheriff. She wondered at the delay but assumed control since she was responsible for the welfare of another life. She gently placed Sophee on the seat beside her in the truck and rubbing her tears away, vowed to care for the baby as her own and love her tenderly and not let the cruel, stingy and arrogantly haughty Gerta cause Sophee any harm by denying her love. She silently lectured Hans for not giving the tiny baby to the kind and loving Abram who would have made a better parent, since she thought Gerta was unable to give love and tenderness to anyone, especially another's child who at birth was pretty.

Hans bathed his wife and laid her out in her best gown. He took his bath, put on his pajamas, looked longingly at his wife, drank his prepared lethal dose of acid, washed the glass and put it away, lay beside his wife and closed his eyes to await his painful, though quick death without leaving any note. He knew he could not live without his Lutricia and especially be responsible for the one who took her life. He prayed his death would appear natural, thus avoiding a scandal for his friends and family to live down. Without his heart and soul, his life was over and too, he felt he could not start over again. He somehow never considered his child who had been given life by him and his wife, she had no rights and by giving her to his sister, he had provided for her.

As usual, Abram handled it all and surprisingly there appeared no gossip of how Hans had died, thanks to Abram, who assured the tenants that Hans wanted them to remain on their farms with same rights and privileges. He drew up new contracts for them to show his intentions. Abram kept the honeymoon cottage undisturbed by strangers.

The will was probated and Gerta received her monthly allowance rather greedily to care for Sophee. The poor baby had a terrible beginning for mere survival. She could not tolerate any kind of formula, neither cow's milk, nor goat's milk, and as a last fight against death since she had lost too much weight, Dr. Lane ordered Emily to find a wet nurse for Sophee. Emily sometimes would take Sophee to the lady's house and some days she picked up the lady from her home and returned her to her home after she nursed Sophee. She continued to care for her own children and considered it a blessing that she could save a child's life. Sophee thrived and made a lifelong friend of Netta Jelks, wife of a black tenant farmer, who worked the fields with her husband so she could help him eke out a bare living, however, they seemed happy to grant Sophee life and Netta gave willingly, since where they were in time, they didn't know a better life for them existed. Emily always came with a box of food to feel better about taking without giving. However, Netta was the only source, ironically, to give Sophee life.

CHAPTER TWO

Emily had become an honest-to-goodness mother which was a full time job. She had given up her practice as midwife and assumed entire responsibility of Sophee who was very fair, with soft corn silk hair and soft blue eyes. She was lovable and charming like her mother and independent like her father yet Gerta never loved her, obviously at times apparently hating her beyond control. Gerta was uncontrollably jealous of Sophee and insisted on piling large helpings on her plate when she first began eating from the table. Gerta insisted on her cleaning her plate by issuing threats and forced her to eat sweets between meals, again issuing threats. Much to Emily's objections, cookies were always offered between meals and fearing being punished, Sophee was eating all day every day.

Consequently, Sophee gained weight and became very obese and suffered horribly as a teenager which pleased gloating Gerta who also forced her to wear long dark skirts and long sleeve white blouses and old mother comfort shoes which made Sophee look older, larger and bulkier but even with all the disfiguring liabilities, that didn't cause the charming personality to fade away and hide behind the fat. She seemed to be waiting and basked in Emily's love. Without choices, one marked time.

At an early age, Emily sneaked her out to her vast holdings and let her visit the tiny cottage. Hans' truck was still in good condition. The tenants learned to love her and with the children she felt free. They were careful never to inform Gerta where they spent their afternoons. Abram arranged the trips and helped whenever he could but even he was afraid what Gerta might do to Sophee if provoked. Since Gerta had inflicted so much pain on Sophee, she wanted to become a nurse and soothe the suffering, so she endured her Aunt Gerta and Uncle Edward's stony silence, her aching loneliness, and her obesity and strangely respected her aunt Gerta by being truly obedient and passive because she thought as an orphan she had no choice and basked in Emily's unselfish love.

Sophee performed with great dignity. She was the class valedictorian because she escaped loneliness by studying and preparing more than the assigned class work. She excelled because she was hungier for knowledge than she was for food since she had always been gorged with unpalatable food. She gave an excellent speech, not appearing to be bothered that her body draped in her academic gown and she extended beyond the dimensions of the narrow podium. Happily no one jeered since her peers loved but pitied the poor fat girl and they had always observed her in that light.

Sophee was considered an eccentric genius who was voted the most likely to succeed. She had always supplied answers to difficult questions on the way in to take tests. Learning was alarmingly easy and she wished to become the professional student by being awarded many degrees since having them would not hurt and they would be hers to comfort and console her.

Abram held off telling Sophee of how her father died and of his great wealth that he had given her for fear of frightening her needlessly and allowing some lowly ambitious rascal to marry her for her money since she treated it very insignificantly. When Sophee told her uncle Abram of her life-long dream of becoming a nurse, he helped her select her new clothes, he paid her tuition and after sending her and Emily on a shopping spree, he let her select her own car, opened a checking account at school for her and kissed her and sent her on her merry way. He felt she was his daughter and he wanted to spoil her by pampering her. Emily moved back home when she was no longer needed but Sophee loved Emily more than her Aunt Gerta and promised to stay in touch. After all, it had always been from Emily that Sophee got her love and boosts when things got her down. Emily would be sorely missed by Sophee who was suffering flight to freedom.

During her senior year at nursing school, Sophee brought her friend, Rick Lamont, home for Uncle Abram's approval but Uncle Abram really surprised her because it was then he told Sophee of her vast inheritance while driving her out to see her estate that she had enjoyed while visiting with Emily. She had made many trips to the farm as an adult but she assumed it was Abram's estate for which she admired him.

Rick jumped at the chance of sharing her wealth. He was so impressed that he proposed immediately and insisted on a June wedding immediately after her graduation. Somewhat dazed but eager to have someone of her own, Sophee agreed. Abram sought to discourage her but to no avail. Emily, Aunt Merle, Jeremiah and his wife, Latrelle assisted Sophee with the quick wedding.

Attempting to get Gerta involved but failing, naturally, Uncle Abram paid for it all, of course using Sophee's money. Gerta let it be known she wanted no part in the wedding since she had never wanted any part of Sophee's life. It was a garden wedding at Uncle Abram's and even obese Sophee made a beautiful bride in her dress of heavy champagne satin and extra long train. Uncle Abram gallantly gave the bride away. Rick's sister, Kate, was her only attendant and his father, Gordon, was the best man.

After the reception, Sophee and Rick left for their honeymoon to an undisclosed destination. Since it was late in the afternoon, the guests departed and left the happy family to clean up and store the many wedding gifts which had surprised Sophee since she considered herself without friends.

While soul searching, Sophee realized she was not any more "in love" with Rick than he was "in love" with her. She endured a little remorse that she had only agreed to marry Rick just to have some one of her own to share a quiet and lonely life and she had no way of knowing that her new husband was a fortune hunter and that without love he was plotting a sure fire scheme to grant him a large divorce settlement out of the marriage charade, thus guaranteeing him a method of allowing him to pick a wife from the many candidates who would fall at his feet just to share his money. With what he would inherit from his father, he gloated at his prospects.

The newlyweds had made reservations at a mountain retreat so after a long and tiring ride, they fell asleep from exhaustion the first night of their honeymoon. They did not share the exotic view from their window overlooking the mountains in their full colorama of splendor with their varying degrees of rich color and hues of the many shades of green. Without love, consummation could wait until morning.

Rick had always had a sexual problem with which he did not discuss with his new bride. He had never enjoyed sexual fulfillment in making love because he was endowed with an unusually and abnormally oversized organ which no woman had ever been able to receive in its entirety, causing him to abstain or masturbate, thus frustrating him. Knowing little of anatomy and being deceived by the enormous dimensions of Sophee's huge hips and large thick body, he thought she was the one woman with great depth and that he could give her all he had with one thrust after the lovemaking began on the morning after their restful sleep. Rick, being rather inexperienced and void of love, without waiting for his bride to get ready to receive him and disregarding her virginity, he violated her and the pain and evident shock was so intense she screamed once and was rendered unconscious. After withdrawing from her, he saw so much blood that he became frightened and tried unsuccessfully to arouse Sophee and through panicky desperation, he called his parents for help.

Fearing public notoriety, they gave him instructions on how to apply pressure to stop the bleeding and warned him not to let anyone see Sophee. They promised to fly up with the family doctor who treated her in the motel room and informed the parents and Rick that her body would heal but he feared her mind had snapped. She lay with eyes open, staring into space. Not trusting Rick's strength to carry out their plan, Rick was allowed to drive alone while his parents and Dr. Spindale flew Sophee back to Rick's and Sophee's new home in Lamont.

Fearing disastrous action from Uncle Abram should he find out too soon, they acted promptly in removing her from the hotel. As her husband, Rick was informed by his parents, that he could do anything he cared to do in securing treatment for Sophee. With the aid of money and with legal aid of other willing authorities, Rick was instrumental in having Sophee declared totally incompetent and under an assumed name was admitted to the state asylum for the insane. He was devastated with fear that someone would find out about what he had done and prosecute him. He removed all identity from Sophee and her luggage and rode along with her and deposited her and her luggage as the legal delegation took care of her admission. He left without showing any emotion other than fear. He carefully removed Sophee's expensive rings from her fingers since he honestly thought she would never need them. To him she was the same as dead. Through illegal dealings, Rick sold Sophee's car.

Rick drove down to Longbranch to determine his legal status as Sophee's husband and if possible claim all the money and property he could by claiming Sophee had deserted him and left him stranded. He wished to recover damages from her family since he had not been advised of her violent nature. He realized he had to attack with surprise and speed before someone found out where she was or until she snapped out of her insane condition. Rick grudingly accepted the fact he could get nothing since Hans had stipulated such concrete plans for any disposition of his land he loved so dearly, and it would always remain in the family that he could never claim as his.

Poor dejected Rick, a victim of his own greed, returned home and secured special permission with a high price to divorce Sophee who had deserted him and was courting before his divorce was final in the short sixty days required by the state.

CHAPTER THREE

Sophee existed. She did not know of anything happening to her and did nothing on her own. She was dressed as all inmates, in a harsh rough grey dress with no belt. While in her room, after the female attendant performed all necessary rituals to be among the masses, she stood in one position in the same corner without acknowledging anyone or anything and when the attendants took the patients or inmates out for exercise, Sophee was led out and stood immobile in one spot and faced the sun. Her fair skin became splotchy with sunburn and blisters which became infected and she soon became unrecognizably ugly and gaunt.

When food was not forced down Sophee, she didn't eat so she began to lose weight. Because of her being young, her skin did not sag when so many pounds were lost. Because of overcrowding and understaffing and possibly her anonymity, she was never seen by the staff doctors nor a psychiatrist. She was not mistreated. She was not treated and was considered hopeless, thus cast aside without care to live as she was until she died.

Sophee never spoke nor demonstrated any emotion. Her time was spent standing or sleeping. The attendants sometimes waited too long to change her diaper so she endured unsightly diaper rash and bed sores but she didn't care and no one else cared, not even her fellow inmates who were as lost as she.

Sophee was hospitalized many months before Uncle Abram's hired detective found out where she was. Rick had written glowing letters to Uncle Abram about how gloriously happy marriage was with Rick, signing Sophee's name but Uncle Abram knew his Sophee and never accepted them as hers. Fatherly love found a way, so he began searching for her. He put in as many hours as the detective. He viewed many unnamed and unclaimed bodies of young women at the morgue. He didn't pray for anything beyond finding her since having her under his protective care, he knew she would have a good life, whatever.

After she was found, he and the detective visited the institution. He felt it was a sterile antiseptic tomb with no love nor kindness, and no communication among staff and inmates. Sophee was terribly dissipated and Uncle Abram immediately had Sophee transferred to a private sanatorium but had to pay for Sophee's room and board before being allowed to take her.

Since her arrival into the unknown, Sophee was examined thoroughly by staff psychiatrists with staff nurses in attendance and she was treated with the latest known cure. Uncle Abram found a quiet place and endured a long cry. He wanted revenge on Rick but considered Sophee's care more important. He prayed for guidance. He received the reports. She still stood facing the corner of her room and the sun in the exercise yard.

Instead of responding favorably to treatment, she began pulling out her hair and pounding her head against the wall while inside, causing ugly sores to form. She was a hideous creature as her glassy eyes bulged and her mouth gaped open as she stood drooling with her head slightly lowered at an angle. To prevent the self-inflicted torture, she was put in a straight jacket and heavily sedated. Uncle Abram found her in this state and threatening the hospital and staff with a suit, demanded and received permission to take her to another sanatorium, very small and very expensive but reported to turn out cured or improved mental patients. It was run by a young psychiatrist who practiced many new and unorthodox methods to bring them back. He cared deeply about all his patients. He allowed Uncle Abram to visit Sophee. He talked to her and cried uncontrollably as he discussed daily events just to talk. He knew he must endure the ordeal because he wanted her to return and function as a sane person to realize all that her father had given her so freely.

After Dr. Travis Zanuck examined Sophee, he ordered her head shaved and the sores treated. He assigned nurses, orderlies and attendants to be with her constantly during her waking hours to keep her from hurting herself after he freed her of all restraints. They talked to her, forced her to walk and kept her moving until she became exhausted. They read to her and made noises in her presence and touched her while assuring her she was getting better. They refused to allow her to stand in her corner and on her spot facing the sun.

After one year of his treatment of generous helpings of tender loving care, tons of medication, thousands of dollars from Uncle Abram and many tearful visits from Emily and Uncle Abram, Dr. Zanuck admitted he noted a slight change, a slight awareness of being a person but at least a change in her condition. He scheduled a session that involved new techniques with a hynotist who was called in to hynotize her and while under his spell, Dr. Zanuck was finally able to take her back to the reason for her condition.

While under hypnoses, Sophee sat up in bed and screamed, "No. No. Oh God, No,", her first words since her mind snapped. She fell back on her pillow unconscious. Dr. Zanuck's soothing voice assured her she would remember and the pain would go away and she would recover. She awoke on cue but screamed maniacally and passed out again. Dr. Zanuck thought she might still be locked away in oblivion where she had been for three years but they were lucky because when she awoke, she endured her first awareness that she could be alive at last. She let her tears of relief flow and soon began her long way back, but she was slow to adjust to normal feelings. Rick's inhumane treatment was beyond her comprehension. She had to learn to overcome her hatred for him since that strong emotion halted her rapid return to good health and logical reasoning, mental and physical. She was shocked to find her rings missing from her tanned fingers. She dared not ask for them because they might not know about her marriage. She would ask later, much later. Time, she hoped, would cushion the

13

blow that perhaps Rick took them. She had many questions to be answered or she could easily slip back to a permanent state of not knowing. She thought the choice was hers so she began to fight for Sophee and her sanity.

The nurses happily laughed at her as she stood quite child like before the full length mirror and viewed the reflection of a total stranger, someone she had not seen in three years, although she liked the way she looked, though puzzled but decided to wait for someone to supply her with reasons for drastic change in her image. Her former long straight corn silk hair was now a mass of short tight curls and Sophee ran her fingers through her hair and laughed. She pulled the curls straight and was amazed to see it so terribly short. She preened before the mirrow in a waiting room and admired her thinness and her first smooth tan which was quite charming. Her ill fitting shift was even becoming on her tiny frame. Being dressed in inmate attire never embarrassed her as she took long walks around the grounds with a nurse and sometimes Dr. Zanuck. They slowly brought her back to full reality and acceptance of where she had been after she shared her traumatic ordeal, however, the why escaped both of them and for that reason she could not be free but refused his request to bring her husband to the sanatorium for questioning since Dr. Zanuck thought he needed care as much or more than Sophee did.

Dr. Zanuck took her shopping for something to wear home. She surprised him by buying faded jeans, pink sweat shirt and tennis shoes because that was what the girls were wearing along the way. He bought her lunch on their last day together since he wanted to tell her he had fallen in love with her and there would, he feared, never be another one to take her place since she was presently a mere child. He confessed he was afraid it was too soon since her mind was still fragile and he was so terribly weak to trouble her with outside emotions. She needed to concentrate on getting completely cured and not on having a confused doctor showering her with his problem of loving her. He adequately confessed his love for her, yet he convinced her there would never be a future for them.

She wanted to tell him he was more than a doctor to her but fearing what she felt was an emotion between doctor and patient and too she had no secrets from him. He probably didn't want a psycho for a friend so she shrugged at the inevitable and silently wished for him to consider her sophisticated and worldy and more than a simple child who could not return his love. She considered herself the stronger one and she knew she was more than what she appeared to be. She remained silent and observed him. Being re-adjudicated created feelings of being pardoned from prison but she felt secure with her sanity and realized Dr. Zanuck was responsible for granting her pardon. Since he had saved her life, somehow he had lost the association between Sophee the woman and Sophee the insane patient.

She still suffered the horrors of what Rick had done and how he had deserted her after professing his love and she knew the going would be rough until she enjoyed the rewards of being a woman, again.

Sophee looked at her clothes that had been packed in her suitcase. She gladly gave all her oversized clothing and honeymoon luggage to the hospital staff to dispose of. Convincing Uncle Abram she wanted to ride the bus home to sort her thoughts took great courage and a newly found strength and willpower, but he calmed down and agreed to listen to her strange request after talking with Dr. Zanuck who, in turn, solicited a promise from Sophee to grant her wish, to send him a post card every month for the next three years as a form of out-patient treatment. He simply could not let her get away, yet. He needed time to decide to win her as his own lady. He probably did not want a patient for a friend especially on his way up the ladder, so, he consciously weighed the choices and wished for her to notice him when she considered herself more than what she appeared to be, but never the person he needed to love, so he accepted knowing he was saying goodbye in person. Being ambitious created hard hearts and demanded perfect, she was to send him a note of her progress on the cards, steps in decision making, from a box of pre-addressed cards, he could accept the gradual loss. She demonstrated great animation as she gave her first giggle, swiftly kissed him and rushed to Uncle Abram who took her to the bus station. Without any word of goodbye, Sophee rushed to get on her bus before crying like a disturbed child again, although she did not remember how she used to act. There were many areas of vacuums and voids she hoped to fill.

The bus stopped many times and delayed its arrival in Longbranch where Uncle Abram was patiently awaiting her. She smiled and hugged him as she said, "Thank you for finding me and bringing me home sane and upright. I love you as the daddy you have always been to me. I pray I never return to a state of not-knowing again. I will work very hard to remain rational and well. Thank you for all that you did for me and for giving me Dr. Zanuck, for without him I would still be an unknown entity. I hope to recoup all facts in order one day. I'll try for you."

"That's all I ask, for you to try. You contributed greatly to your return. I pray I never have to shed so many tears over you. I love you but I hope you decide to assume some of your financial responsibilities, even if wealth never seems to interest you. Your father would not understand, so take inventory and decide your future. Until then, stay well and happy and know that I love you like the daughter I never had."

"Please continue your patience. I shall make a suitable decision as soon as possible."

"Thank you. Anytime you want to see the books and visit your estate, I'll arrange a proper tour of everything. Plan to give me several days before your departure."

"Agreed. Now let's face the monster my father gave me. I hope he never finds out how sick his sister has always been. No offense, just stating facts as I see them. I'll give you a week and thanks."

Sophee was frightened at being responsible for so many people, so much land and so much money. She hoped to satisfy Uncle Abram but she knew she could not remain on the farm. She could not work as a trapped woman with so many inherited responsibilities but she would be gracious in her threat to vacate the premises.

When Sophee went in search of her wedding presents, she found none. Denying Gerta the chance to gloat over their disposition, Sophee assumed all were either sold or given to someone else. She refused to cry over more of Gerta's inflicted stabs of inhumane treatment. She didn't need Gerta nor the gifts since both were heavy responsibilities and she needed neither of them.

CHAPTER FOUR

Being back home in Longbranch should have been richly rewarding, but it was very difficult for Sophee, sometimes almost impossible. Aunt Gerta had happily informed everyone in town whom she met that Sophee was crazy and bragged that she apparently had always been, therefore people who had always known her and whom she considered her friends had grown afraid of her, especially her friends' parents. They dodged her when she met them on her way to Uncle Abram's. They inquired about her ability to find her way around town, insisting she needed someone to care for her.

Since Gerta was afraid of her, she remained locked in her room when Sophee was in the house, but Sophee spent most of her time with Uncle Abram and at her parents' cottage which remained as her parents had left it, seen to by Uncle Abram. She felt at home there. Applied therapy of cleaning, painting and polishing restored good feeling and her lovely home, making another bedroom out of her nursery as every one called it, because it was built for her. She found solace in its stilled silence which forced her to consider changes in her life.

She spent many happy hours on a motorcycle touring her large estate. The tenants admired her and respected her presence; however, she never meddled in their affairs as Uncle Abram had organized. She felt compassionate toward her tenants so she forced Uncle Abram to issue ninety-nine year leases with a ninety-nine year option renewal on ten acres of land on which their houses were built and for his exemplary manner in which he handled her large estate and the way he rescued her, she gave him the same deal to a club house and land on the river where he longed to spend many happy hours in retirement with Merle. His son, Jeremiah had taken over most of his practice and had learned how to manage Sophee's estate so she rewarded him with a beach house. She gave Netta and Brent Jelks the deed to their land and house and gave them a large financial settlement. She bought Emily Jackson a town home and gave her a large lump sum settlement. She felt she had rewarded love. Money meant nothing to her because she felt it betrayed her when Rick learned of her enormous wealth. She accepted enough money to operate on and the check books Uncle Abram gave her. Not feeling that she belonged since she was only at home at the cottage and being denied employment because of her confinement and Aunt Gerta's betrayal, she decided to leave town. She gave Uncle Abram his promised time and convinced him and Jeremiah that she was fit and sound and capable of making it on her own, even after finding out from Uncle Abram that her father had committed suicide rather than remain with her. It troubled her deeply and she yearned to call Dr. Zanuck to help ease the pain and soothe the fear that she had inherited his traits of self-destruction.

Saying goodbye was easier than she had anticipated. She tucked her travelers checks, personal check books and extra spending money along with her "prescribed treatment cards" already stamped, in her surplus olive drab shoulder bag and then tucked two pairs of faded jeans and shirts beside her few personal items and tennis shoes. She wore a heavy purple wool shirt, purchased from a thrift shop, over her faded jeans and draped an old grey woolen poncho around her. Around her head she tied a colorful headband which changed her entire image, which she had wanted to achieve. She dusted off her comfortable walking boots and left the old hometown that had never granted her happiness and by hitchhiking, apparently fearing nothing. Strangely enough this lack of fear frightened her which threatened her confidence. She needed her doctor but she had to make it on her own, along the way. Nothing happened to her. Nothing to frighten anyone. With her soft blonde curls almost hiding the headband, she looked too innocent to risk going to jail over. In her frame of mind she wanted little of what her daddy left her so she resorted to an exciting and dangerous life of a vagabond. She was searching for her way back to a normal life and yearning for its recognition when she found it. She reprimanded herself for allowing herself to be driven away by foolish whims of people who condemned her for having been mentally incapacitated and still deranged frightened her into believing she had inherited her father's weakness in preferring to give up and go with the one who loved him and whom he loved rather than stay and be richly blessed by the love of a child, the gift of lfe, who would have made his life more fulfilling than what he accomplished by deliberately destroying it and crippling her emotionally. She prayed she would find herself and the answers to all her "Whys" and achieve enough maturity to take charge of her legacy left by her father. But for now, she could not remain where she was and attain her desired goals without leaning on Travis, the man, who was so utterly entertwined with Zanuck, the doctor. What if she would not recognize her answers and still seek them, only to keep bumping into them and dodging, rather than analyzing her confrontations, sorting and adapting the ones which suited her. She had cried over being considered useless, worthless and unsuited to pursue happiness in vocation, avocation or love.

Becoming a rebel might not be the preferred way to meet life head on but Sophee was determined to find a way for her to survive life without hurting even if she crashed head on before she found that intangible for which she was searching. She had everything, but in essence, she had nothing. No place to hide without involving others and no place to cry without alarming others so she chose to run since there were no restrictions on what pace or how far to run, half way there and half way back. It comforted her that she made the most logical choice. She wanted more but didn't know actually what it was she wanted. Turning her back on all creature comforts which were available to her in great abundance was a coward's retreat but presently being endowed with great material wealth and responsibility was beyond her ability to cope and adapt to her father's way of life and live off the land. She had been robbed of three valuable years of her life and she now wanted to march in double time to catch up with some of that lost time but not among civilized mode of living.

Because of a heavy rain, she hailed the next bus to a strange city where she joined a group that represented what she was seeking. The members of the group called themselves hippies. They were seeking shelter from the rain at the bus depot and congregated around her since they thought she was one of them by the way she was dressed and all alone, with little luggage. Liking their friendliness and openness immediately, when asked, she joined them. Being naive and new at becoming a rebel and wishing to attach herself to someone, she trusted them but in circumspect she was impressed with their leader, Mitch Hawkins, older than any of them but definitely in charge, their reverred leader. Being alone was terribly frigthening so with a respected leader she was glad she had accepted their invitation to join them, doing what she had no idea but she was among humans and in that there was security.

They informed her that the townsfolk condemned all long-haired hippies and with that knowledge of having their threats carried out by enforcing the laws by locking hippies up for vagrancy or any trumped up charge, the group with Sophee entow, left in their packed open truck, that was literally wired together. They were exposed to all the elements, but Sophee soon found they eased their discomforts by sharing one cigarette that was passed around which she soon learned to call it what the others so lovingly did, "a joint." She feared that any foreign substance that would put her out of control might push her newly gained sanity over the rim so she refrained but secretly wanted to take flight with the others. She bought her first pack of cigarettes and learned to smoke but thought the others derived more pleasure from their smoke than she.

Seeking the permanent but temporary location to camp, they camped under the stars until they found what they were looking for—uninterrupted peaceful existence. They found their Shangra La, a rural setting which was beautiful and each chose his own living quarters in the deserted rambling weatherized frame home that had four fireplaces but only one bathroom which they soon expanded with primitive johns in the woods. They spread their sleeping bags, set up the camp stove, gathered wood and kindling to start their fires to warm up the damp place which smelled of being empty. They began supper of pinto beans, stale bread and beer which was always around even when there was no food, there was always their beer and their joints. No bedroom furniture was needed since all except Sophee carried their bedrolls on their backs.

Sensing her inexperience and fear, Mitch tossed her an extra blanket and invited her to bunk beside him until she decided to choose someone to share his bedroll or choose someplace else on her own. He guaranteed her safety if she remained with him so she felt secure by his side. She smiled at him and thanked him for his gallant action because she knew she was a prime target for the young single men who would pursue her, which she reasoned was natural and in a weird sense, quite flattering.

Sophee, the rebel, began a way of life totally foreign to her former protected one and accepted her survival as theraputic administrations prescribed by life. Each member pulled his own share of the chores and never did more than was expected and each got some kind of "funky" job making enough money to barely survive but that's all they wanted, daily comforts with lots of free time for pleasure of all kinds. Everyone worked for cash to prevent establishing records of employment which could be traced. Sophee stashed her money in an old beat up purse some former occupant had left in the dwelling. She held on tightly to her checkbook, money and travelers checks so no one would find one and cash it and set a trail for the authorities. She trusted all of them but decided to leave nothing to chance. She had not gone far enough yet.

The house took on an atmosphere of home with old discarded pieces of furniture brought in, repaired and set up. Pictures from magazines were tacked on walls. Heads and bodies were checked daily for lice and scabies, which if found, created total isolation for the victims until cured and area sufficiently sanitized. She found the group to be respectful of truth and deeply loyal and the reasons for banding together, or at least one of the reasons, was to protect a few who for personal reasons refused to sign up for the draft, especially since war was never declared. Even after the president created the lottery to entice young guys to register, the gamblers chose to escape backing an issue in which they did not believe. Some radical members were against everything that anyone else stood for. They were deliberately bucking the system but were non-violent and law abiding citizens. A fine male specimen, a healthy and strong member of the group, about six feet four inches tall, starved himself to be declared unfit by being underweight however, it caused permanent damage to his health which denied him a chance of ever holding down a job. Several friends were victims of freak accidents while experiencing new highs. Jerry's and Phil's bodies were found in Jerry's car, dead as a result of sniffing menthol spray. The group always banded together and viewed the "planting" of their loved ones whose destiny had been given them through an effective and thorough grapevine system of communication. They always returned to camp to get completely splattered or stoned because their friends knew that was what their departed friends would have wanted. All jobs were forgotten until the proper period of mourning had passed. Somehow they could always find another menial job no one else wanted. They asked for little and expected less from a society they had learned to distrust and for some actually to hate. They forgot, that when normal days returned, after all they said and did, America, would still be theirs and she would treat them with the same respect as all the others with open arms.

The young men who were on the dodge lived in mortal fear that some patriotic or revengeful person would turn them in as traitors. Their battle was faced every minute and Sophee felt their war was similar to battle for them since it was much harder to face what they were attempting than for the others who went where ordered by politicians and faced enemy bullets. Both deadly odds of battles, being planned behind desks at the home front. Even after the president who blundered was replaced, amnesty was granted; those who had run kept underground barely existing and daring not to fall in love and make plans for their future. Either way all lives were devastated by the conflict and some recuperated sufficiently to go on with their lives while others never left. The conflict and its era remained in the minds and hearts for many. It was hell either way for those who stood and watched and for those who fought and died and those who lost more than the others, their minds and memory. Sophee empathized with the sufferers of real and imagined nightmares of having to face such harsh and real decisions at an age of not being old enough and yet all were branded for life since they were never convinced the suffering was necessarily theirs. Couples lived together without marriage and they reasoned that as long as birth control prevented pregnancy, marriage was not necessary. They reasoned it took more than a piece of legal paper to hold couples together and the joy and convenience of living was greater than planning for the unpromised tomorrows.

Striving for homey atmosphere, radios, stereos and television sets were in evidence and many loud selections were playing constantly. Several members of the group were talented and the concerts were entertaining. Many attended concerts in distant cities hitching there and back and always surprisingly returned. Sophee bravely learned how to cook a few dishes and to live comfortably among the tribal family. She forgot about herself as she joined their communal rituals. She sorted her thoughts of wasting her nursing talents but she enjoyed the basic act of living and earning money from her work in a greenhouse. Her tight curls clung tightly to her head when she started sweating but nothing phased her except an occasional snake which was declared harmless. She displayed her creative art in preparing hanging baskets which were her aesthetic contribution to the family, who praised her vociferously for her creative ability.

By way of the same excellent grapevine system of communication, many traveling hippies consequently dropped by frequently for rest and free meals, since they always knew where they would find friends. The young men were sometimes quite horny and on occasional nights lodging, the hippies sought the first available female for relief. Sophee was forced to take showers with Mitch to prove she was his woman to convince the visitors she was not available for them. She dreaded an anticipated fight which would probably have brought in the law, so she obeyed the unwritten rules and jumped in and kept her eyes shut tightly, strangely enjoying the intimancy, her first shared shower.

Mitch was a perfect gentleman and friend and laughed at her fear and embarrassment, although he had repeatedly guaranteed her safety with him because he revealed he had left a vital part of him back on the battlefront but he never explained to her and she was a cowardly friend and afraid to ask for the details. She eventually accepted his explanation as fact.

They were close bosom buddies, the first one in her life; therefore, she enjoyed and cherished the close relationship and she depended heavily on his sage advice and friendship as he tutored her in the many ways of being totally committed to his way of life. She reserved a part of her independence but accepted their teachings and beliefs on the surface and somehow was never kicked out because many saw through her facade. She abided by their code of living and revelled in its strange logic of total freedom and peace and truth. She grew and expanded mentally and emotionally and rejoiced in her classroom of life with many teachers and the heavens as awarders of grades.

Sophee survived the many nights that demanded her demonstration of belonging to Mitch but slept so closely to him during the nights of the visitors, that he could not turn over without crushing her but never shoved her aside. He enjoyed being her protector and sharing philosophy with her. While expressing her asserted belief to anyone who cared to listen that she was her own being and was briefly detouring from responsibility because of a temporary breakdown in her acceptance of who she really was, she vehemently exclaimed to argumentative perpetrators to stand back and keep their distance or endure her defensive method of survival by shouting to them that if they didn't like her peaches not to shake her tree, so the onlookers respected her privacy and took her as she was without invading her territorial rights.

Hopefully life among the hippies would grant her peace and the strength to shed her defeatism and allow herself to grow and develop into a worthwhile person. She prayed that her struggles would at least bring about some remarkable change. She had learned to relax in their presence so she felt she had a good chance to change.

When Spring came, they put in their organic gardens and actually harvested vegetables which improved their daily lot of potluck meals and their secretly hidden prized plants provided them with what they needed for extended pleasure trips and escapes. Thankfully they were never raided, even though the local legal authorities suspected them and cruised through their compound.

She had sent her cards to Dr. Zanuck without a return address and had kept in touch with Uncle Abram and Emily without telling them where she was, what she was doing or with whom she was living. She knew they would not condone her way of living and also Uncle Abram might send the law after her. She still had not been gone long enough. She was still searching. Also, she had not gone far enough.

CHAPTER FIVE

After her free life style of many months, she had regained enough personal strength and determination to make it on her own since she was very stable, sober, talented and sane. She knew she must leave her friends because she wanted to expand and grow and not just hibernate. When they discussed disbanding and going home, she thought of doing something with her life. She wanted to walk in the security of Mitch's shadow without having any input into her future so she knew she would never find herself under his protection; therefore she knew it had to be on her own, so she waited for the perfect time to enter the mainstream of life and find what it offered her.

While they were checking out the old battered truck and loading their necessities, Sophee made her departure which hurt. As she had left Longbranch, she now left her classroom, hitchhiking in the same clothes, older and more faded and badly stained jeans because she needed nothing more. She was wiser but had forgotten to look for herself since she had been so very busy living. She left with no regrets and all seemed happy to be moving on; however, giving up Mitch created a new low of her own in her life. She chalked it up as another loss, part of her destiny and required little adjustments.

No names nor addresses had been exchanged. There were painful goodbyes and each knew their paths would never cross. The peaceful camp looked as if nothing had been disturbed. They hocked what worked and burned pictures on the wall and dumped what didn't really work at the trash cans.

Hitching into town was not tiring. She bought a ticket for a town she had wanted to visit since she wanted to put miles between her past and her future where she planned to work for a while at her profession. Blitchfield had very wide streets and many cars were parked in front of shops and stores and many people were busily getting to where they were going. She felt she had chosen wisely. Her one tiny room at the "Y" suited her. She converted one corner into a kitchen and used the bath down the hall.

While exploring the city, and looking for ideas for her possibilities of change of employment, she located a college for nurses and after investigating and overhauling her appearance, she was allowed to study for her state board exam which was required before going to work. Her portable skill was a blessing in that she didn't have to ask anyone for money or handouts. Strangely she decided to use what she had brought with her and never considered using any of her inherited wealth. It was as difficult to remember all the medical information the second time as it had been the first so her spare time was devoted to preparation with alarming speed which guided her through the dreaded time of acute loneliness.

She passed the state board and was hired to work on the third shift in the emergency room of a very busy hospital which she really liked. The bazaar cases astounded her and she learned more at work than she had in school. She made many friends but never allowed anyone to get close enough to break her barrier. She was an enigma to all the staff because she didn't attach herself to anyone and lived as a poor church mouse although her pay provided her a higher style of living.

No one at the hippie camp would have accepted the astounding renovation but she soaked up all the culture and was happy when her little shopping spree wrought change and acceptance. Her co-workers finally accepted her little idiosyncrasies. She never revealed her hippie activities nor any part of her past. She was a lady of the present only.

There were many women in uniform, especially nurses which interested her. She saw them about town and they intrigued her. Usually she saw them at the post office shipping boxes. When Sophee approached them, they informed her they were leaving for their tour of duty near the battlefront where nurses were in great demand. Her mind came alive as she realized and accepted her ordained destiny. She went about collecting pertinent information about receiving military training for nurses for which she felt qualified. After training and pulling a few strings to expedite her departure, she was on her way to the battle front and suddenly she knew her purpose in life was to be there whatever the consequences and she yearned to let Dr. Travis Zanuck know of her plans but could not. She almost waited too late to decide because of her age but she was elated at having been accepted. She failed to mention her stay at the mental clinics because she knew only people of stability could endure front line hardships and since nothing was asked of her, she left it where it was. She considered being an unidentified Jane Doe remedied not spilling the beans. She was sane and adaptable so she played her cards with a new deck and actually prayed for a change. She looked quite trim in her uniform and her newly cut very short curls guaranteed a perfectly saucy look with her officer's cap. Any candid eye could see she was an appealing model for the recruiting posters.

Giving up her cubby hole existence was a delightful chore; however, saying goodbye to Uncle Abram, who convinced her that how she viewed him while at home would be her last since he knew he would be gone when she returned. Nothing deterred her since she felt so strongly that she had been called to serve her country where she and her fellow nurses were so critically needed. Jeremiah pledged his continued loyalty of making her vastly wealthy and to keep Uncle Abram alive if possible. She visited Emily and spent a few happy hours in her cottage but decided not to spoil her final visit by seeing Gerta. She was ready to depart and face her new challenges. Uncle Abram drove her to the depot and waved to her as long as he could see the train. She was not ashamed of her tears. She had earned the right to cry.

It didn't take long for Sophee to realize that hard and constant work and sometimes impossible tasks were the order of the day. She had to quickly and efficiently adjust to the change in climate and weather, the difference in hospital administration and the alarming statistics of death and survival plus exhausted vigilence.

Being a nurse was standard equipment for facing and accepting gory sights but Sophee had to find a space to "spill her guts in private areas" upon arrival until she became toughened to reality of war and what it promised. She often wished the casualties had been mechanized so new parts could have been snapped on in exchange for those shot off in battle and lost in booby traps thereby restoring the young fighters and nurses to their original form of life or most often mere survival. She was ashamed of her cowardice when the victims demonstrated greater dignity than she when she first arrived, but along the way, she found a way to survive and endure and perform the duties she volunteered to do. Keeping up with her duties kept her too busy to wonder beyond their survival. At the hospital she recognized accurate and quick fixes and observed with all her being. She realized that "War was really Hell." But one had to be in it to really know that war and all its ramifications were all about her with nary a spot to escape it if she dared.

After escaping certain death so many times, she was nicknamed, "Captain Blarney Stone" because they reckoned her safety was guaranteed from having kissed the blarney stone itself. The name was shortened to "Stone" and soon no one knew Sophee Tillers existed and she was excellent with the confused ones awaiting orders for shipment to the states. She and the other nurses and doctors were good Samaritans who served diligently and willingly. When an emergency arose which aroused all, the call went out to get Stone. Some days she never knew more than a couple of hours sleep at one time, but she was overworked as all the staff and rarely complained. They accepted their new way of life and purpose. Her purpose was to restore peace and quiet as soon as possible without disturbing the other patients, by calming or removing disturbed patients, temporarily out of it.

She ate the prepared chow and smoked too many cigarettes but her greatest blessing was that she never feared for her sanity. She knew she would not probably return too easily to being a vegetable. She was following orders and knew or hoped she knew she could endure and perform as well as or as long as any of them but she felt her hopes were more often borderline while suffering fatigue. She played hard when off duty and recouped her strength to begin the never ending cycle.

Her conscience was bothered with nagging thoughts of the battle of facing the traumas but she would have been relieved to learn she was a well put together nurse whose thoughts differentiated between Travis, the lover and Zanuck, the doctor. She never engaged the others in talks her heart was waging. Doctor—

man-doctor and unfortunately she never chose one over the other. To help clarify her dilemma, of Travis, doctor and Zanuck, doctor, she began sending notes to him. At first only her name, then simple words like, "Here." "Troubled shadows." "Me and them." "Winning." "Me." and finally leaving off name and signing "Me, at last." She hoped he interpreted her inferences correctly. She did not wish to alarm him. Fearing a forced R & R or a return trip home, when she realized she was safe at last with no threat of crumbling, she kept her silly game to herself and prayed the man would win in the battle of choosing him over needed doctor since she still considered herself his patient since she owed him her sane life. In the newspaper, <u>Lamont Sentinel</u>, that Uncle Abram had always sent her, Sophee was shocked and saddened to learn that poor misguided Rick, her husband of one day and night, through extreme depression over being turned down by the military services because of an unknown heart condition, had driven his car onto the train tracks and parked, awaiting his untimely death which was granted when the speeding train hit his car and dragged it for two hundred and twenty feet, apparently causing instant death. She wept for him, because he too had been a victim and obviously never sought guidance to learn to live with his problem that to some may have been a great treasure. Somehow his death alleviated some of her suffering but she continued to wonder why she had been so miserably treated because of ignorance and shame. He had never remarried which brought no further emotion. She rushed a letter off to Uncle Abram that she accepted the information without additional suffering since he wanted her to know about Rick's death and not something he used to frighten her. Uncle Abram's love had always sustained her but she often wondered why she could never enjoy love with any man.

CHAPTER SIX

The replacement doctors and nurses were easily spotted when they hesitated briefly at first about making snappy decisions and carrying out the suggested techniques under emergency situations. They only hesitated once and soon became experienced pros. Sophee spotted a new doctor coming on duty as she slowly proceeded to her bunk after sixteen hours on her feet and merely nodded at his greeting.

After two short hours of sleep, the call came out for "Stone" and the new doctor was hurriedly dispatched to fetch her immediately. He found his way to Stone's tent and cautiously touched her and whispered her name, "Stone. Stone." and was totally surprised when he recognized the short curls of "Stone" as Sophee's as she pushed aside her net, jumped into her "suit of armor" and ignoring who her messenger was, headed in the direction of where she was usually needed after hours. She empathized with them because she vaguely remembered being in an insecure condition but was at ease with knowing where she had been. The young man in the extreme corner was upsetting the other sleeping patients by screaming very loudly and not allowing anyone to come near him. Sophee walked toward him to find he was crying and screaming for his mama to help him. Stone sat on his bunk and soothed him in her frightened but experienced manner as he whispered to her, "I dreamed mama was in a boat which broke into and mama drowned. I swam very hard to reach her but I did not make it. She smiled at me and disappeared. I am scared to sleep. I might dream again. Help me."

"What is your name soldier?"

"Sam."

"Okay Sam, let's get you in the shower. It will relax you and you can fall asleep easily. I'll remain with you until you sleep. Please stop your screaming because the other roommates are sleeping."

"Okay. I am sorry. I forgot where I was."

She motioned for help, still ignoring the new doctor who observed her in her impressive action. Very unobtrusively the orderly took Sam for his shower while she rolled the wet bed away and replaced it with a dry one without arousing suspicion. Sam never knew she wasn't his mama. She held his hand until he slept. She turned to exit and squarely faced the beaming Dr. Travis Zanuck and fell into his welcomed outstretched arms which enveloped her. The sheer joy of seeing each other was unbelievable as she quickly backed away and hastily explained who "Stone" was as he commended her for handling the situation so calmly and efficiently and so very compassionate to avoid embarrassment to the young man.

27

He walked Sophee to her "home" and after soliciting a promise from her to see him later, he reported for his initiation.

They were friends at last. They enjoyed their stolen times together. They discussed her notes to him which he had understood. To further explore their feelings, he convinced her to take R & R with him after he had completed his assigned tour of duty.

Feeling guilty at leaving when the demands of their sheer strength was overpowering, she was very excited to have two whole weeks of rest and relaxation with Travis who was troubled by his mixed-up feelings for Sophee. She had demanded separate hotel rooms for the exploratory test which he quickly sanctioned.

It was almost beyond her depth of logical thinking to witness the daily hubbub of normal living and happiness when she had just left a full raging battle of death and dying of all peoples there. No one seemed concerned that men and women and children were being killed in mortal combat with the known and unknown enemy. She paced her movements with the residents and tourists and watched sadly as the relaxing GI's were walking arm in arm with their mates who had been flown in to help them recuperate, only to have their man return to battle and perhaps death or disfigurement. Presently only the hour was considered which they shared, forgetting yesterday and dreading tomorrow.

It seemed to Sophee that she was perhaps the only unhappy one so she set out to snatch as much happiness as possible with Travis and forget the war like the rest. They were happy and content. Their days were spent leisurely in exploring the island in a rented car and flying to an adjacent island to view the pageant on the history of the people and the islands, and luxuriating on the beach and imbibing exotic drinks at the many bars. They enjoyed glorious highs. They stood in line to get into clubs, especially one with a singer who accompanied himself at the piano and engaged lovely hula dancers who livened up the show.

Browsing through the many stores and looking among the glamorous mumus and gayly designed sports clothes excited her. To blend in with the crowd, she bought them matching shorts and tops. Browsing was more fun than shopping since she had so many selections to choose from.

Travis, sensing his valuable time for exploring his feelings was fleeing too rapidly, requested room service and had breakfast delivered to his room and invited Sophee who cautiously joined him for a quiet interlude and delicious breakfast. Perhaps it was the setting, his bedroom or the lovely view of the beach, palm trees and the water from his window that prompted her to relay her well plotted thoughts to him. He merely smiled as she asked him to make love with her because she trusted him and knew he understood her plight. He need not know that she was afraid that she loved him. Her fear was overwhelming that she would repeat her performance and snap if she renewed her sex life. He cradled her in his arms and promised to make love when she was ready since he could sense her fear. He wanted their union to be perfect so he waited for a sign from her; however, it took great courage to deny her. Their days were passing very quickly and nearly at the end of their vacation, she knew she was strong enough emotionally but she thought she needed false courage, so she drank constantly to stimulate her, but it destroyed her charm and cheapened the anticipated pleasure of having her as his own, so he allowed her to sleep it off and he kept his back turned away from her repulsive gestures in attempting to appear in control. She was ugly and repugnant but he hoped her drinking was not a bad habit with her since he knew very little about her, the person, while he knew all about her, the patient. He felt he was in Hell and was being forced to make a decision to remain there or seek love elsewhere which he knew was impossible, but commonsense demanded that she could never survive in his world and there was no place in hers for him.

She had taken a bottle to her room and when she was gloriously high, she went to his bed and upon awakening found nothing had happened between them. Travis explained he wanted her to know him and to enjoy the pleasure of two people in love. She returned to her room, comforted her hangover with more drink and wallowed in self pity but in the end, cherished him for being so thoughtful. Later it was he who came to her room. He was tender and gentle as she slowly became a woman; however, without pleasure since she was denied an orgasm. Her inexperience did not allow her to fake pleasure so Travis was disappointed and so was she but didn't let him know since she did not know how to tell him fearing a deflated ego. She was thrilled that she had succeeded in making love which to her was a near miracle. She had survived the crisis and she would not go back to a life of no feelings. She held the sheet tightly under her chin and cried as Travis accused her of only wanting to perform the sex act with her doctor as mere therapy, not that she could love and be loved as he continued to dress. He further stated that he had simply been her device which she had used unfairly because it was as a patient she succumbed to her doctor and not to the man, her lover. He reminded her of her confession of making a choice between man or doctor and he coldly stated it was apparent the doctor had won. Remembering his oath, he extended his medical expertise to her if or when she needed it in the event he had impregnated her.

Rejoicing at being made angry as well as being ashamed over her inability to reach an orgasm, she called him an antiseptic coward and an uncaring weakling with no feelings of the male animal. She also accused him of being the confused one and promised to take her loose bolts elsewhere and assured him she needed no future calls from him, to which he merely responded a curt goodbye and explained he had to hurry and get home to begin his search for a woman who could love him for what he was, a vibrant man, and not for what he promised psychologically. He smiled, causing her intense pain as he explained the choice was very elementary and not one to be pushed out of proportion as she had done.

Love was more than a sex act. To him it was the total commitment of perfect enjoyment and pleasure when two lovers became one. He somehow judged her on his terms and found her lacking so he did not budge from his stupid belief and pushed her and his love for her out of his caring and resolved to search for somebody who acquiesced to his charm and desired the same pleasure as he. He had been her shrink and failed to associate her ineptness at sex with her trauma of being actually raped. He sought only his pleasure and condemned her. If only she had the courage to deny his hold over her which enslaved her, nevertheless she succeeded in dodging Travis before he left.

He had closed the door softly as he slipped from her. She picked up her bottle and began her downhill slide to self destruction by finding pleasure that drink offered. She managed to complete her hitch without working drunk while on duty but she endured steady hangovers and when her enlistment was up, she considered staying in, but her dependence on the bottle was too great and she knew she could not be responsible for saving lives in her drunkened condition, nevertheless, she could not go home either. A nut was hard to endure but becoming a drunken nut was impossible to her yet she felt she could not stop by herself.

She settled for a cheap and dinky apartment on the beach in a strange city a long way from home. It did not take long for her to sink to the bottomless pit of degradation.

She drank alone in her ugly apartment and when loneliness was unbearable, she frequented bars and woke up in strange beds with strange men, not ever knowing how or why she was there. She never enjoyed sex but continued to allow herself to be picked up. She never went on the pill because being prepared for sex insinuated that she was promiscuous so she pretended all was safe and she was a proud lady. On one such occasion she enjoyed her first orgasm and surprisingly her partner extended his stay beyond the weekend. From that moment of great pleasure, they spent equal time at each other's apartment with nothing in mind but good sex. She forgot her bottle as she devoted her mind to the thrill of enjoyable sex. He was a salesman and on his final two weeks of leave before returning to work, so they honeymooned and rejoiced in their shared happiness.

On one of his return visits, she shared the news with him about finding out she was pregnant which created great turmoil for both of them. He severely scolded her for letting it happen. She resorted to her passivity and said nothing about it being as much his fault as hers. Since she was educated on birth control, she was guilty. He resolved the situation by proposing marriage since he felt he could never be responsible for denying his child his name. He insisted and succeeded in convincing Sophee it was the only way out. Buying a suitable beige gauze dress and espardrilles after registering their bond and getting their license and blood test, created a festive and happy mood; however, she was unprepared to accept his actions of going directly across from the Judge's chambers at City Hall where they were married into a lawyer's office and filing for a divorce. Her marital record of one day only moments later stood before the sound of their vows had gone. He gave her a large amount of money to pay her hospital bill and made her promise to receive excellent prenatal care to guarantee their child a good life. He threatened to keep vigil over her so she would stay away from booze, bars and men, hopefully dodging dangerous diseases to be transmitted to his legal child. He kissed her goodbye and explained that although she was the best partner he had ever had in bed, without love in a marriage, sex had no chance to make it stick through the ordeal of living together. Being "Miss Humble Pie", she merely said goodbye and thanked him for the great sexual fulfillment he had given her and especially for her child. He calmly walked away but dropped in occasionally to determine her health status and finding her in good condition he soon left, not desiring even sex from her. He explained his family never would allow him to surprise them with a secret wife in a strange city and not know her pedigree since he was the heir to the snobbery of first families of America. Drake Koodack was a proud man who assumed responsibility for his act and for that Sophee admired him but even with his child she could not stay married to him. She asked him, "Is there any condition that you could surprise your family with a wife?"

"Yes, if she were rich, no questions would be asked. Too bad you don't qualify. I like playing house with you. Why did you ask?"

"Curiosity, only. I thought perhaps there was another qualification."

Seeking energy to survive, she took long walks along the beach and the warm sun on her face reminded her vaguely of a time when she depended solely on the sun as her only contact with the outside world but she could not remember when nor where she had been during the familiar ordeal.

Luckily for Sophee, Drake, her ex-husband, dropped by to check on her to find her on her way to be delivered. Eric Hans Koodack arrived without complications but Sophee was exhausted after fourteen hours of labor. Drake drove her home and remained with her until he felt she could care for both of them. He even stocked her larder with food for both of them. He promised he would never seek custody and that she could put Eric Hans up for adoption if she cared to. He was hers to keep without any bother from him. Eric Hans didn't possess the required pedigreed blood lines to Drake but too, he didn't investigate which he might have been surprised at his findings.

Sophee was a good person at first but when the newness wore off and she had lots of idle time on her hands, she again turned to the bottle for comfort and solace. She drank just short of passing out so she could care for her baby but she was rapidly falling to a low state of devastation and she worried about Eric Hans. She feared for her sanity and loss of health, but continued downhill without trying to break away from her habit and reform. She was thankful she had not returned to bars and men. She was about to exercise her rights and end her life of goodness. She needed someone other than Eric Hans to comfort her.

Sophee endured a strange awakening when she met Claire Swanson, a semi-retired nurse at the upper end of the beach where she had strolled with her baby in her arms. Sophee felt she was dying since it took both hands to held her drink, steady, acute diarrhea was always there and she stank. She only occasionally ate food and her malnutrition was showing. She could not think, yet she continued to drink. Her savings were dwindling and she felt lonely and depressed. She tried to keep her baby well fed and clean though she did it as she described her feelings to her child. Sophee was walking along the beach letting the waves splash over her feet when she felt that old familiar sense of comfort that haunted her and brought a pleasant realization. The warm sunshine brought peace because she still vaguely remembered that she had depended on the sun as a source of escape at some time in her past.

After that eventful day of meeting Claire, she began walking every day a little further and finally met her at her beach shack. They shared their problems and recognized each needed the other. Claire was an alcoholic with five birthdays of sobriety. Claire became her mentor and Godmother to Eric Hans. She succeeded in drying Sophee out but with great difficulty and restoring her to good health as a functioning human and reunited her with her assertive attitudes. It was Claire who convinced her to go home. Sophee and Eric Hans looked healthier with Claire in charge. Sophee accepted Claire's suggestion as a challenge by taking Claire with her to help care for both of them.

Sophee's self confidence had always been weak and fear of failure and intolerant of her dreaded incompetence destroyed her faith in herself that she could care for her and her child alone among people who considered her crazy. There was still a narrow margin between her alcoholic dependence and sobriety; however, she wished to remain sober but more than anything she wished to completely overcome the desire for the destructive liquid. Somehow her child did not arouse the drive to become a caring mother and devote her time and talent to lavishing him with the love she never had. She did not know how to give love since she had no knowledge of ever having received it from a mama, yes, from Emily and Uncle Abram which she appreciated but still suffered. She dammed all the circumstances that caused her to be what she was and failed to accept any wrongful part in not learning how to cope and to change.

Excitement grew as they made preparations for departure and change. They gave up their apartments, tossed their personal belongings into Claire's bomber that didn't promise a safe trip to Longbranch and hit the road. Eric Hans was secure in his bed in the backseat. Claire was utterly disgusted at Sophee's appearance in her old faded jeans, scuffed boots, out of shape sweatshirt and head band and army jacket, but Sophee explained that was the way she left so it behooved her to return in same manner, after all, she was a bonafide lunatic, thanks to Aunt Gerta. Claire demanded the dignity of being mother but Sophee went as she was.

Serving in the war zone, the notoriety of Rick's death or the presence of a child, pushed her to a realm of respectability in Longbranch. She, Claire, and Eric Hans moved into her parents' cottage and through Claire's guidance, Sophee decided to upgrade her image by creating an extravagant wardrobe, straightening, styling, and dying her hair red. She joined many clubs and allowed her position as vast land owner to become known since she owed a legacy to her child, Hans. Jeremiah was very happy to have her in as assistant and hoped she would assume command since she needed to invest her large holdings.

Jeremiah's son, Jason, would take over for his father since he also would be a lawyer. Simply to demonstrate her power, she bought a three hundred and fifty acre farm on which was a rundown house that resembled a large school house and many out buildings, frontal highway footage and a large pond reportedly stocked with fish. Uncle Abram and the faithful tenants helped restore the house and property and she and Claire filled the house with antiques. Eric Hans' nursery was lavish but not impractical since he would soon grow into a boy and then as a man. Sophee offered Claire the same deal as her other tenants by operating the farm as her own, guaranteeing the taxes and insurance if Claire would care for Eric Hans as her own until she could attend schools to learn how to manage her farms and how to invest and to operate everything she owned so she could assume the responsibility of Eric Hans and become a good mother but she was afraid that would never be and moved in a young farm girl to care for Eric Hans.

To Sophee's chagrin, Claire accepted and shocked Sophee by starting a sheep farm which actually worked but all tenants were not happy about it. Sophee was bored by such calm existence. She enrolled in an accounting class and a management class which involved four hours daily. She soared through and enjoyed learning something new. She poured over the farms's books with Uncle Abram and Jeremiah and amazed them with new ideas. With Eric Hans in good hands she enrolled for further training in psychiatry which she loved and applied it on many unsuspecting victims.

Since learning was easy, Sophee decided to get a BS degree in nursing and teach when she made up her mind what she wanted to do. She wanted to find out the status of Travis Zanuck on his turf if possible. She needed to straighten out her life and make a stand at the farm or in a hospital. His hold over her forced her to turn down all male attention and she was rapidly getting too old to play games. She had sought counselling and wanted to determine if it worked since some of it had been absolutely shocking. She had come a long way and wanted to have another chance with Travis since she had failed so miserably the first time. He never tried to see her so she assumed he was definitely not interested in her but he had to tell her that. She was tired of carrying the lighted torch for a myth which didn't console her and hold her when she cried.

CHAPTER SEVEN

Uncle Abram and Aunt Merle died about a year after Sophee's return. She reasoned they had waited for her since they felt she belonged on the farm. She placed them beside Hans and Lutricia and felt they would be happier together in death as in life. The shade of the cedar was a beautiful final resting place for the Tillers. An iron picket fence was erected with a gate. The cemetery was landscaped resulting in a secluded and happy place which she could visit without hurting and where she could talk to them.

She missed not having known her parents and wondered if she would have been less passive if they had lived. She had finally forgiven her father for deserting her because she knew the power of love and the foolish things it caused as well as its complete consumption. Her dark days of drinking troubled her but she had been thankful that she hadn't resorted to picking up men during her sprees after Eric Hans came along. Her alcoholism hopefully would be an act for forgiving and forgetting, but she had to find Travis, one of her other sins to find out if he could condone or condemn her and learn what her feeling promised if anything.

Getting a job at Dr. Zanuck's Clinic was very difficult. She submitted resumes, requested interviews, and dropped in to fill out applications. Either to cease her constant vigilence to get rid of her or because she was truly qualified and was needed, she was hired to work in the pediatric wing.

Following Claire's advice who brought Eric Hans to see her often, Sophee dined at the prestigous restaurants attired in the latest fashion, attended the opera, the same church as Dr. Zanuck, the country club and participated in tennis and golf with abandonment. She plotted her image building strategy of being the most suitable choice as the wife of a successful doctor since she wanted him to notice her in some way, if not in bed where she had performed disastrously and ended up losing him, then in her expensive apartment which was almost more than she could afford on her salary.

During the rounds he failed to recognize her as a redhead so she demonstrated great efficiency and pretended she also was the stranger since she had begun using her child's name. At staff meetings his eyes wandered toward hers as if in wonderment but he showed no interest in her. Not recognizing the name nor her, he stared at her name tag as he ordered her into his office. As she entered, she blushed, and then he finally recognized her as he continued asking her to meet him in his office to discuss new patient treatments he had recently learned about at the medical convention in Europe.

Daring to break the barrier of doctor, nurse, she asked one evening, "How have you been? Did you make another trip to the battle zone?"

"You are Sophee. I thought I was hallucinating since you pretendeded not to know me."

"I was hiding behind my new name and my red hair since I thought you never wanted to see me ever again, after what happened between us."

"It took me awhile to get over the feeling of being used, but now I understand and I am sorry to have caused you any unhappiness. You are looking great."

"Thanks. I am divorced with a five year old son. I have come a long way and have made many mistakes but with a good friend by my side to keep me straight, I shall survive."

Looking at him and being near him after so long a time, she rejoiced, she was over him. Hopefully it had been a clinical association of dependence compounded with fear of being incapable of having sex. Drake had saved her and had given her a son. She must thank him by taking his son for a visit. Sophee struggled with her emotions to keep her feelings under wrap as he enthusiatically explained the outstanding statistical report of the success of the newly applied techniques. He seemed to be sharing his enthusiasm with an equal. He ignored her as a personal friend and made no sign he had known her intimately before. They communicated on their clinical level of comprehension awaiting a sign of interest of old feelings for a brief moment. She experienced butterflies that she no longer cared and wanted to know how he felt about her, yet he remained the professional. She was hurt at the realization that he wanted nothing from her but she again asked, "What do you feel for me now, other than an employee?"

"When I first saw you, my pulse throbbed and my heart beat more rapidly but to me, thankfully, you are that, an employee, nothing more. Are you comfortable working her with me?"

"Yes. You are simply Dr. Zanuck, of which, I am glad. I had some bad times, but now I am free. I can work here without any repercussions."

"Thank you for being honest. I guess I am a good doctor, at least, and not the lover I once desired to be. Good luck. The staff think you are an excellent nurse so should you decide to leave, get a letter of recommendation from all of them, including me."

"Thank you. I must return to the floor. Goodbye."

"Goodnight."

She returned to her floor and mechanically performed her daily duties until her shift was over so she could have a good cry over her final acceptance of losing her mythical love. Even though she no longer loved him, she had been rejected by him without any remorse. The hurt was very real and nearly devastating but she was truly thankful to let it go and attempt to get involved again.

Without any explanation, Dr. Zanuck triumphed over Travis, the lover. Sophee endured her trauma of again being personally rejected, but along the way toward maturity, she had learned how to cope so from here on in she would possibly become her number one priority and win at the game of love with an equal partner.

Her daily existence of becoming someone else just to get a little recognition had caused an attractive person to surface so her ordeal was not in vain. She liked the person she had become and decided to keep the new look. Turning to her child who was now at an acceptable stage but unhappy that all his questions couldn't be answered would bring new challenges to her simple life or after all she could resume her legal duties in Longbranch and give him the good life she never knew.

Her resignation brought only a mere goodbye from Dr. Zanuck but in the following Sunday's paper was the announcement of his wedding to a young and beautiful socialite who had what he evidently wanted. Sophee was spared any further painful confrontation because of her quick departure to Longbranch. She hoped to devise a plan to accept her true feelings of not caring for someone who nonchalantly informed her she no longer counted even if she realized her emotions had changed. She felt discarded, dirty and cheap and it hurt. She wanted to be let down honorably and gently, not as a discarded stethoscope. She pledged to assume her place as mother, friend, and owner of Tillers Estate, her child's legacy and her yoke.

Sophee's timing was uncannily productive and most appropriate, seemingly planned. Shortly after her arrival and settling in the cottage, Claire lowered the boom on her by announcing she had been approved and was in the process of adopting eleven children, six girls and five boys, who had been orphaned recently with no known living relatives and the children requested not to be separated. She insisted that Eric Hans would fare better with her and the other children rather than with his real mother since he had been with her since infancy. Sophee helped Claire rearrange her house to guarantee as much comfortable living for all as possible. Carpenters performed the necessary duties to add on and renovate, and the huge old house soon looked like a dorm by granting privacy but additional baths were installed reducing space. Most of the children were in school and time was crucial in getting a turn at one bath. A large antique dining table of solid oak was brought in since it seated twenty-four people at once. Eric Hans, Sophee and Claire bought everything the children would need as far as household furnishings and large nightshirts for all and saved the grocery shopping as a get-acquainted spree; however, Sophee thought there was a safer way than having each child to select his or her favorite food. She could picture the pandomonium caused by the ruckus but she planned to be there to have Eric Hans make his choices known since he was still Claire's child and on rare occasions Sophee's child. Hopefully the regular shoppers would have completed their grocery shopping and only the employees would enjoy the experience, especially of ringing up the huge order of groceries.

Sophee plunged in completely and enjoyed the rat-race of preparing for the children who had been in the orphanage since the death of their parents. Eric Hans was a dear and ate hastily prepared sandwiches and was so hyped up over new brothers and sisters that he had trouble getting to sleep on time and awake early in the morning. Fortunately he was never grumpy and Sophee enjoyed getting to know him. For once in her life she felt in her heart that she had decided to keep him with her and learn how to be a mama. She felt she had made the right decision in reclaiming her child and living on the land, that would one day be Hans', but she also felt she had waited too long because he still called Claire mama and turned to her for his needs, so she knew what fate had in store for her. He accepted Sophee as a good friend and was confused that he was to live without his real mama, Claire, but somehow he never questioned his situation because of the clamor of making so many changes. She was suffering alone.

The big day of decision finally arrived. Hans begged and was granted permission to ride in Claire's new station wagon to the state orphanage to claim her brood. When they arrived at the orphanage, out stepped the director, television crews, local radio, newsmen, photographers, newspaper reporters and cameramen and the dazed children. The cameramen began snapping pictures of the children as Claire hugged each child while keeping Hans by her side since she actually felt he was truly hers. Everyone was happy to pose and responded shyly to the many questions. The children gently tossed their bags of clothing into Sophee's car and filled Claire's to capacity. All the staff had hugged the children goodbye. Hans, since Eric had been dropped from his name, looked like one of the other children and Sophee somehow knew he would never be hers because of the competition and Claire's devotion. The time for claiming Hans had passed and history could not be undone. The record stood. He now belonged to Claire who apparently understood what motherhood was about.

The residents of Longbranch and Darrow County had brought dinner for everyone and set up tables where the excellent home-cooked food was piled. Claire, in a few short years, had easily become one of them while Sophee was still ostracized even though she was filthy rich.

As the children stepped from her station wagon and Sophee's car, several children from the welcoming group who were of each age snatched a child and friendships began. Tosca, who had been hired for Hans' care, took over the care of Tabatha, the baby. Hans was at home with all the adults and neighbors and soon was shouting and screaming like the rest. The land and love of it had won but she felt no sense of loss.

Claire, in every sense, became their new mother when, after the crowd had dispersed, she restored order and assigned rooms, each child to have single beds.

Hans looked at her longingly and Claire's eyes met Sophee's over his head as Sophee nodded assent for him to be assigned a roommate. He never thought it necessary to say anything as he ran with his new brother to his new room.

The ceremony declaring Claire their legal adoptive mother was private and beautiful. Sophee cried but her tears were brought on by complete happiness. The children could begin a new school with a new name without mid-year changes. The legal system and Drake had cooperated satisfactorily.

Many people cried as they sat in their pews and watched as Reverend McFarland baptised Claire, Sophee, and the Swanson children: Joseph, Anna Marie, Ernest and Martha, twins; Morgan, Ruth, Hollis and Sally, twins; Trent, Eric Hans, Ruby and Tabitha as Uncle Abram's family stood as sponsors. Each received the right hand of fellowship. Sophee was touched and hoped to maintain her faith. She knew Claire and the children would have no problem.

Accepting her cowardice, Sophee was grateful that she no longer had any moral obligation to keep her in Longbranch except the land and she prayed it would remain in safe hands. She regretted that she could give up her child so easily and with little regret because she knew she could never meet the requirements for farmer or mother. She felt a deep abiding hate for the land's power, and hoped her hate would eventually dissipate. She again plotted her course of action by again leaving her comforts and material wealth to search for the hidden part of her that she really didn't hope to find but would enjoy the course her destiny would lead her while meeting life head on with an open heart and mind in accepting what life offered.

CHAPTER EIGHT

Somewhere along the way, Sophee would find her pathway to complete restoration and peace where she could apply adhesive qualities to evoke a permanent way of life that did not interfere with her fragile though free spirit which refused to settle for tranquility, while seemingly learning to endure all advantages and disadvantages that her choice of life dealt.

She was in charge, and the comfort of her well-established legacy in the Tillers estate and Claire's sheep farm motivated her to venture since she would always have something to rope her and bring her home, but to this she had always rebelled and sought a different and better life but always meriting the same amount of self denial and loneliness.

Letting her natural blonde tight curls become her new hairstyle and reorganizing her practical wardrobe, Sophee was about to leave home one more time. Before finding a home away from home, she bought a small sports car and pulled out a large sum of money after preparing her will whereas she left her entire estate to Hans with allowances to provide for Claire and his eleven new brothers and sisters with Uncle Abram's grandson as executor of her estate. She considered at least one would become another farmer with the love of the land her father possessed and develop the estates prosperly although Uncle Abram, Jeremiah, and Jason had done exceedingly well by its steady progress and enduring prosperity.

Sophee's destination was a large hospital where she could expand her knowledge of the mind and help return trapped minds to their original form. By having been on both levels of performance along the way, she had much to offer and she knew that she could never function as someone other than a dedicated nurse. She was happy with her new method of leaving Longbranch because it was with pride and dignity that she waved to the best friend she ever had and her children who granted complete and unquestionable love and acceptance which Sophee was able to return at a distance. She rushed forward to find her new life.

Although panic struck as she drove directly toward the sun while unholy and frightening memories after being rejected by the one who healed her sick mind and wounded her loving heart, engulfed her, causing great remorse and a deep yearning of belonging to someone or something or for her same old habit to help her overcome and allow her to abide by her newly found faith in the land, especially in hers, and in her child or rather Claire's child, and in her friend, Claire, who gave her her soul and in her future, sustained her as she lowered her windows and enjoyed the total abandonment of reality and caring as her thoughts soared. If only she could enjoy the legacy because her financial future was very secure where she belonged—in Longbranch. Her treasures and traumas were safely stored in Longbranch and she was guaranteed a final resting place as she hurried toward another beginning, frightening but absolutely accepted. Her sane mind and healthy body were awaiting her destiny along the way. She patted the steering wheel to the tune on the radio and sang along as her plans unfolded.

No one would ever know how good it felt to be free of all hates, hurts, and rejected love, even though this feeling of love never let her enjoy complete bliss because without a tug of reality along the pathway of living, there would be no challenge to strengthen her. She refused to allow the tears to fall but knowing she could feel, sustained her, after Rick's treachery, Travis' desertion and Drake's awakening her passion to feel and enjoy. Since she had plodded along a terribly rough road to awareness, she dreaded knowing the narrow margin between the two. All roads led to where she wanted to go and to what she wanted to be and merely to be along the way and completely alone.

Checking into a motel with pleasant design, she felt more alone than ever before in her life. The next day, boredom, fear and home-sickness attacked her. She kept remembering Claire's words. "Return home since the land and Eric Hans are what you are seeking. Feel the soil in your hands as well as in your heart and under your feet. Plant your roots here." She called Claire and pretended happiness.

After making up her mind to give the land, the children and Claire another chance to convert her, Sophee returned home and no one chastised her nor laughed at her decision. She had made everyone happy, especially Claire, who loved her completely even during her periods of ambivalence since she had come a very long way back.

Sophee assumed the role of friend and assisted where she could. The circus was very exhausting but exciting to watch the pleasure on the kids' faces.

After an exhausting day of taking all of them to the Travelling Three Ring Circus and getting all of them home, fed and in bed, Sophee, very tired and dreamy, and Claire were enjoying a cup of coffee laced with honey, relaxing before falling in bed. Claire interrupted their comfortable silence. "Now that you are back and hopefully for good, what have you decided to do about Hans? I know the adoption is legal but as his mother, I am certain you could reverse that since his father doesn't seem to care what you do about your child."

"Claire, my decision was final. Hans is yours for life. I came back this time, but the next time, I might decide to leave during the day or night. I am not certain of any longevity at any place."

Claire smiled at her, "I think you have some more travelling to do before you settle down and scratch all your itches. Thank you for endowing me with his future. He is as much mine as the others and he feels like one of the kids."

Sophee looked thoughtful, "Claire, Hans needs to know who his father is. He is a fine man and comes from an established family. Hans would like to know that since you will give him stable security. We will fly up on the next flight out, if that meets with your approval and return after a few days. He won't miss school. He is such a smart student."

"When you decide to do something, you don't mess around, do you? You don't need plans nor do you have any doubt he will be right where you expect him to be."

"You are you, thank goodness. I am I and can leave on short notice without any plans on either end. He agreed I could do anything, that he would not interfere. He thinks I am scrubby poor as far as something about proper bloodlines with no class nor culture and in other words, not in THE BOOK. He approved the adoption by signing the paper your lawyer sent him so he is at same place still. When I see him, I'll present him my current financial statement. It might shock him to find I lease out nearly twenty thousand acres of land and reap the proceeds from nearly three thousand acres, my stock portfolio and banking investments, plus all the houses, animals and equipment which has never meant that much to me until now. I will flaunt it to let him know I can match any pedigreed spouse he has chosen to share the prestigious name of Koodack which represents first families of America. We came to America later than he but we rank among the elitist and richest and we were among the elite of our region that daddy left for a better life here. Especially me, the whore he married and divorced because he assumed I had no good bloodlines, but he gave Hans his name. I am overflowing with great riches with you as a good friend who plans to mother our child, the heir to all this. You have him but he must inherit what is mine and I guess I'll share in the lives of him and his siblings. I am anxious to see Mr. Koodack again. I can't go overboard since he did a gentlemanly deed in marrying me."

Claire sipped her coffee and asked, "Did you love Hans' father?"

Sophee snickered, "Lord no. I met him the morning after I took him home with me from the bar. Or, he may have taken me home with him. It didn't matter. We enjoyed great sex, my first, after getting over what my husband did to me and a failed attempt at sex with my shrink, Dr. Zanuck, whom I thought I loved, as you know. Drake and I were perfect together. He only married me to protect his child's name and filed for divorce the same day he married me. He took care of us financially, not knowing I could provide that. I did not steal his thunder. I hope he still lives in Scrobell where I plan to begin the search since that is where letter was posted. How about you Claire? Surely you have had a great love or two?"

Claire shrugged, "Yes. One great love which was more than enough. We were both bottle dependents who could not be weaned. We were married and as far as I know we still are. With all the publicity the adoption has given me, he will probably show up one day and I'll probably take him back if he wants me. I sobered. I hope he did. He was the hospital administrator where I began my nursing career. Our love was deep and our passion like wildfire but strangely, no other man has lit my fire."

"Why haven't you divorced him?"

"Why should I? I like my life as it is but if he wants to resume our married life together, I'll take another chance on him. We punished each other, both physically and mentally so each would be taking a chance but our love for each other deserves that chance. We could have no kids so now I could give him a houseful and he would love all of us equally. He is so giving in that respect. Frankly, I have considered looking for him but have been too cowardly to risk another failure. I have let God and nature rule, so I don't worry about our tomorrow. I met you and through you I almost have it all. I cherish our friendship."

"So do I. If I had not met you, I would have lost both me and my child. Thanks now, but I hated you when you forced sobriety and decent living on me. You are one strong and determined lady. I am glad to have you as a friend whom I love and respect very much."

Claire touched Sophee's hand, "You have given me a great purpose in life and I plan to always remain a trusting friend for you wherever you may decide to roam. When you get halfway there, return to me and what you have here since this land and Hans are what you are seeking. Never shut the door on what your father gave you. Cherish it as he did and plant your roots. You got a raw deal in the beginning as well as the rest of us. Shake it off and feel the soil in your hands, as well as in your heart and under your feet."

Sophee smiled, "Thank you Reverend Swanson. You gave me that advice when you were trying to convince me to come home. Your very words brought me back home this time. I shall give those words much thought when I leave again searching. That's enough at one sitting. Book a flight out as soon as possible while I prepare Hans and me for departure. We rushed through the adoption so we can do this."

Claire did not move as she continued, "I appreciate the Tillers influence and money. I wanted the children to be adopted and wearing my name and to possess a baptismal certificate before they entered school so they would be spared unnecessary hurts and unanswered questions. Their parents were poor and proud and were killed in a stupid hotel fire so they are of good stock and with my name and your money and influence, they will have a good heritage to live up to. I had to say that since my tongue is loose. I'll book a flight out tomorrow but for now, Goodnight."

"Goodnight Claire. Should I be negligent in the future about saying I love you and God Bless you, remember, I am thinking it. Hans and I will leave the day after tomorrow. I am in no rush. I have to make necessary preparations, papers, you know."

CHAPTER NINE

Sophee knew she was being melodramatic and extravagant but she merely wanted to convince Drake she represented what he wanted. He might consider her a fool for not telling him but she felt she was not in a convincing situation. The matching luggage was unnecessary for one trip. Their expensive clothes could be utilized at the expense of buying the other eleven similar attire so Hans would not stand out as being the only expensively well dressed child out of the dozen offspring. It would be worth it so Sophee planned to spend more of her money.

She fastened their seat belts as the plane prepared to land at Scrobel Municipal Airport. Not knowing how long it would take for her to find Drake, she took the motel room for an indefinite stay. Hans was excited by the sights and sounds of the large city and at meeting his father, as he exclaimed, his real father. He accepted that Sophee was his real mother but Claire was his real mama. She hoped he would not be hurt but the kindness he had shown in wanting to give Hans his name, gave her hope that he remained the same caring man. She knew the lawyer had sent the paper back immediately which meant he was the same man she had met and enjoyed. She wanted to see him for old times sake and to show off being rich since Hans was totally content with Claire and apparently did not yearn to leave her for his real father.

Locating his office with the third phone call created a little excitement. Sophee left a message for Drake to call her. He was due in his office next day and while they waited, she and Hans browsed through the city and enjoyed being together, eating junk food and loving the freedom of non-conforming to strict home rules. For the first time in her life, Sophee had gone all out in creating the right look of success and she had no doubts that she had succeeded. She needed a bit of assurance, so looking in the mirror in the motel room, Sophee was satisfied with the reflection of a very attractive, well-dressed and well-groomed young mother and of her handsome son as he stood quietly beside her.

Sophee smiled at Hans as she asked, "You think we will pass your father's inspection?"

Hans smiled as he replied, "Mother, we are not being put on the market to be sold. Relax. I am I and you are you and after we meet my dad, we will still be the same two people. We are gorgeous and yes, mother, we both pass inspection."

"Thank you. You have hidden talents and I guess we'll never know their genetic source. Let's be on our merry way. I love you for many reasons and all I want for you is your complete happiness. Don't shut the door between us even if you are to be Claire's son forever."

"Mother, you have nothing to worry about. I'll always be near you, but you can't stray too far so I could never find you. I love you, too."

Sophee hoped she could follow Drake's direction for their meeting. He was meeting them at "Lems", a restaurant near his office building. Its nearness to his office and safety piqued her curiosity. She reasoned that his experiments with sex away from his home town were now haunting him since she and he had been total strangers and their relationship never revealed more than their satisfied desires. She was a tiny lamb as far as being experienced in the real world but he was probably wishing that he had never adopted the habit of frequenting bars for pick-ups but it was too late to worry about what he and she had or had not done. The day of reckoning was about to be reconciled.

Sophee was enduring a strong urge to flee. She felt her body had betrayed her by responding to Drake's potent lovemaking but she heaved a deep sigh and proceeded as directed. She smirked at the thought that perhaps Drake might wish to make a quick exit, using his old established office as a safe sanctuary. She also thought perhaps he might be assuming she wanted his money since their agreement had not been in writing. She mentally chastised herself over her thoughts. He had no reason to see her. He could easily have refused. Her body had chosen wisely, Drake was and would always be an honorable gentleman of whom Hans could be proud. Hans possessed good genes, and with Claire's excellent environment, he would be a contented and contributing member of his world.

Acknowledging that it had been a long time and having nothing between them except a healthy and shared sex appetite that gave them Hans, he was entitled to see his father if at all possible. Even if Hans would never be a part of his future nor hers, he had the inalienable right to know him and make his own choices. Sophee had decided to keep Hans' destiny from his father. She dared not risk challenging the crankiness of the human mind. Hopefully she was removing all potential cobbwebs of doubt about his heritage that he might have inherited a self-induced insecurity of unworthiness and fear of lack of mentality and that he might be an offspring of some parent who might be a contributor of bad genes that led to physical or mental breakdown. She wanted Hans to know his father represented security, good looks, health and propriety.

They spent a short while in getting a cab but it took much longer to get through traffic. Sophee smiled at Hans as they entered "Lems". Drake was waiting for them so by giving his name to the hostess, she was spared the ordeal of recognizing him. She smiled as she realized she would not have had too much difficulty in spotting him since Hans bore a strong resemblance to Drake and it was easily recognizable. Drake stood as they approached his table. He had not changed, just aged a little and his maturity added to his demeanor that shouted, "bloodlines". He shook her outstretched hand and smiled broadly at them as he spoke. He looked greatly relieved. While looking from one to the other he managed to finally speak, "Hello Sophee. I see you and I produced a handsome son if not a workable marriage. Hello Hans. I suppose your mother has told you about me and who I am."

Hans smiled and stood taller as he timidly answered, "Yes sir. She told me you are my father who signed a paper so I could be adopted."

So much for her desire not to tell Drake that his son would not be in her care. Drake breathed deeply and looked at Sophee, "Yes, son, I am your biological father. I agreed to the adoption because no one else can claim that honor. I thought perhaps your mother had remarried. Your mother and I were divorced before you were born because of the time in which you were born and impossible circumstances, that of traditions and legacies and selfish pride, prevented me from being a father to you."

Hans never blinked nor shed a tear as he asked, "You mean you did not want either of us?"

Drake paled as he replied, "No Hans, it wasn't that I did not want both of you, but that I couldn't stay married to your mother and stay in the good graces of my family because of inherited silly traditions. I thought it best not to fight since I would have lost both you and your mother and my legacy of inheritance and my anticipated future of owning the Koodack empire and all that it extends to me and my family. I made the selfish decision to give up both of you to spare you the ugly involvement of having to go to court to keep you and losing all I cherish, the Koodack legacy for which I have been trained. It had nothing to do with you personally. My parents protect the family circle by selecting and approving their children's mates to guarantee good bloodlines to carry on in the Koodack tradition of possessing pure bloodlines. Your mother, I thought, could not be approved while we were on the West Coast where she lived and where we met and married."

In the silence of accepting facts of not quite being good enough to be worthy of snobbish traditions, Sophee opened her large purse and pulled out her latest financial statement and the complete researched Tillers genealogy from the country of her father's birth and that of her mother, the Hepstart family, as she gloated, "Relax Drake. We are not here for your money and since you informed Hans that only you had been endowed with perfect bloodlines, the great Koodack legacy, here are my most current financial statements, and my genealogy provides excellent qualifications to enter us in "The Book". I made this trip expressly for you to meet your son and to inform you that you could have kept us since we do come highly qualified and are properly registered on both continents."

Drake's eyes held hers as he opened the packet of papers and while he was perusing them, the waiter interrupted him to take their order. When he was satisfied with the facts, he looked chagrined but smiled at Sophee as he raised his eyebrow and said, "Why didn't you present your case then instead of now?"

Sophee's eyes never left his, "I did not think you would believe me, considering the events leading up to our marriage and quick divorce and subsequent birth of Hans. Your mind was programmed for the proper marriage sanctioned by your parents and nothing, not even the facts you are holding, would have mattered at that place and time and that particular woman."

Drake sipped from his water glass and held eye contact, "From your situation then, I would have thought you were lying to keep me or that you were a fool since an appropriate wife could not possibly have been there in your prevailing and unholy circumstances. You know what you represented then, to me, at least."

Sophee pulled her eyes from Drake's and looked at Hans who accepted his dad rather nonchalantly as she asked, "Hans, do you wish to ask your father any questions?"

Hans looked closely at his daddy as he asked, "Are you married now?"

Drake smiled at his son and a pleasant look crossed his disturbed features, "Yes. I have been married for several years to a lovely lady, Fedelia. We have two children, a girl, Asta, and a boy, Drake, III, whom we call Trey. Would you like to meet your half brother and sister and step mother? You have grandparents also."

Hans looked searchingly at Sophee and then looked directly and a bit harshly at Drake, "No sir. That's all right since we'll never meet again. My mama who adopted me does not wish to traipse all across the country to have me visit a man who never wanted me as his son since you have never seen me. I have seen you and have been informed of what you prefer and you have seen me and know that you made a mistake by not keeping us. It ends here. Thank you for being so very kind in seeing us. I know now that you could have refused. You have your family and I have mine. I don't want to hurt your feelings and burst your bubble but having a dad does not count all that much with me. I hope you understand."

Drake chuckled, "I am glad I could meet you. I am proud to have you as a son, but if you do not wish to be troubled with the necessity of travel for us to visit, I understand. Anytime you feel like checking up on your old dad or if you need me, you know where to find me. Please call and stay in touch."

Hans smiled, "Same here. If you need me, you know I'll be at the Sheep Ranch on the Tillers Estate with my five brothers and six sisters, all adopted like me. My mama, Claire, will be there too but I don't know where my mother Sophee will be. She loves to keep moving, but at least she still comes back."

Drake asked, "What's wrong? Don't you like motherhood?"

She fidgetted briefly as she answered, "Yes. I love being a mother, but staying in one place is my problem. It puzzles me. I have been involved with school and work at a hospital out of town necessitating me to leave Hans with a friend. It is better for him to have Claire as his mama since she stays home with her children while I merely visit."

47

Drake said, "Hans, it seems you are in good hands with two mamas, one stationary and one travelling but two who love you."

Hans looked at both of them as he answered, "Yes sir. All of us are usually happy."

Drake smiled, "I am glad to hear that. Thank you for wanting to see me. I like being a father."

Hans looked soberly at Drake, "Thank you for seeing us. I guess you are my stationary daddy who stays away like my travelling mother."

Drake drove them back to their motel in the company limo and as he stood beside her, he said, "Sophee, why haven't you remarried?"

Sophee looked at him and said, "I don't like marriage. It is too confining. I don't even date. I love my son, even if he is no longer legally mine. I feel free to leave when the urge to run is too strong to deny."

"Try it with love next. time. The shared love may surprise you."

"No. I don't like surprises. I like to feel free to move at a moment's notice without getting permission. Marriage is not for me since my residence is never guaranteed."

"You could buy you a husband. Your money would keep him happy and you could roam where you pleased."

"Drake, money does not motivate me. I find having money to be a problem, but I would never buy a husband. When I plunge, he must want just me. Love and I are top priorities now that I have secured Hans' future by giving him a mama who loves him and sees that he is properly cared for as to his necessities for survival. That was cruel. I don't deserve such dirty thoughts, especially about marriage."

"It's good to see you have become quite a lady. I can easily claim you as my former wife whereas before I shuddered over what had happened to me and where I had planted my seed. Thank you for letting me see our son. He is a lot like me—proud and stubborn. I can accept his not wanting to be a part of my life. I admire and respect his honesty. He will have no trouble in making a place for himself in the world. You have done well for both of you. I am proud to know you."

"Drake. I have always been a lady. I met you during my temporary days of rebellion. I don't know where I'll be during my tomorrows but whatever road I take, I'll travel it alone. Don't worry. I know what I am doing, where I am going and also know how to return. People do mature even without growing up."

"I wish you happiness and success at all levels of endeavor. Goodbye Sophee." He hugged her and turned to Hans, "Thank you again for coming and may you always have the best in life. Goodbye son." He hugged Hans and looked into his eyes.

Hans spoke, "Thank you and goodbye."

On the plane as Hans looked out the window, he said, "Mother, thank you for giving me a chance to meet my father. I can't love him. I hope I am never as hooked up on bloodlines as he is. He made me feel a little tainted that even though I am his son, he can't claim me yet I could wear his name and still use his blood which can't be changed. Sorta weird, you know? Blood is blood. I love you for letting me become a Swanson who claims plain and simple blood for all simple persons."

Sophee was hurting that she had been relegated to nothing since in becoming a Swanson, he was no longer her child and a Tillers legal heir unless she chose to recognize him. She swallowed her hurt and breathed deeply for composure as she said, "Even with plain Swanson blood and no famous bloodlines, I wanted you to know who he was to erase all doubts about who you really are. You don't have to fear rattled skeletons in your future with Claire. Now, I am glad to know you never had to wonder who you are. You are Hans Swanson, pure and simple. Thank you for being who you are. I love you. I hope you learn to love the land as your grandfather Tiller did and can help to carry on his legend that he left with me."

"No promises mother, but I don't believe I'll be a sheep herdsman."

They both laughed. She would try not to cry until she was alone and safe at home. The experience had been overwhelming and exhausting. She wanted to stay on the plane and keep going from one stop to the end.

CHAPTER TEN

Enroute home from the airport, happily cruising in her red sports car, Sophee and Hans witnessed a three car smash up, involving serious injuries. Accepting her responsibility and civic duty as a nurse, she asked if she could give any assistance. While she was giving aid to the injured, the ambulance driver commented, "Ma'am I wish you could become a magician and wish a hospital wing here in Longbranch to take care of this kind of head injury and the other patients like him. We will have to take him to Longbranch General for them to get him prepared for survival and travel for his trip to Willow Memorial, about two hours from here. That is a long way with dangerous speeds to safely transport a critical patient. Anything can happen to make it a one-way trip to the promised land."

Sophee helped with the injured while Hans stood near and watched since she could not leave him in the car she had left on the side of the highway. Yet, he was not disturbed at the sight of blood and unconscious and seriously injured patients.

The man's words haunted her. After dinner at Claire's when the house was quiet and time for Sophee to go to her cottage, she asked Claire, "Is it difficult to build and operate a hospital if you have the needed capital?"

Claire looked for signs of flight as she answered, "No, I would not think so. Why? Got another itch?"

"Not to leave. We were at the scene of the reported accident enroute home from the airport which involved a serious head injury. The caring ambulance driver stated that Longbranch General did not have the facilities to treat the patient. If that is true, then this old town needs another hospital. How does "Tillers Memorial Medical Center" sound? I have never spent much money and it sits there and makes more. Instead of investing in the stock market, I could switch to real estate. It's time for me to realize what I inherited."

Claire looked closely at her and asked, "Are you serious?" Seeing the determined look on Sophee's face, she spoke, "You are."

Sophee nearly screamed as she exclaimed, "Yes, Claire, my dear friend. Tillers would be quite appropriate."

Claire smiled and took a deep breath, "And you would be tied to it which would keep you here, for awhile at least."

"Would you please give me the names and locations of the best hospitals that have the facilities that we will need. Since you keep brochures of hospitals you would want to work in, just in case you decide to leave Longbranch. I am not the only person who gets itches. I am glad you now have the sheep and the children to hold you here so Hans can have a home and a mama who lives with him. We'll check them out and go from there."

Claire licked her finger and raised it, signifying her secret was out. She gathered pad and pen, looked through her collection and began writing. She handed the list to Sophee as she said, "Here are a few of the very best that offer every kind of treatment, especially for head injuries and for children. If you need me for anything except floor duty, call me. You will perhaps hit the road tomorrow?"

Sophee laughed, "Yes, but you knew, I suppose. I'll be out of here first thing. I am taking a lawyer who Jeremiah is recommending."

"Good luck and I pray for your safe return."

"Thanks, but what I really need is a miracle and perhaps gumption to pull this off. I must like hearty bites of challenge."

Claire smiled, bursting with pride, and said, "The lack of both never slowed you before."

Sophee laughed and left. After making her decision, everything else seemed easy. Jeremiah assigned Drum Pollard, a lawyer in his firm, to accompany Sophee to protect her. His notorious reputation of loving and leaving women didn't phase her. When he insisted on driving his personal car, she smirked at his threat of dominance. She considered him safe and single since she was prepared to return to Longbranch in same condition in which she was leaving. He definitely would be safe from her. It was her expedition and she was dedicated to bringing Longbranch citizens better care.

They were taken on long tours of many hospitals until Sophee made her choice of combinations. She thanked each team who had given her their time and professionalism and promised to contact them later. Instead of returning home, she located her design architectural firm and negotiated with the company to supply her with specifications and drawings. She gave them a few of her personal requests. The price was discounted since they felt charitable. They beamed when she gave them her check for partial payment, and she smiled when they seemed surprised.

Drum was very charming but had a bad habit of eating in swank and expensive restaurants. She enjoyed having him with her to lend his masculine influence. He catered to her whims and let her know he was a virile man and available.

They returned to Longbranch to solicit sponsors. Tillers' Estate bought more than enough land which had to be sold as a unit. It was located just outside the city limits and had access to all utilities. Sophee became a new person and accepted cooperation from firms and furnished only small expenses to hook up to water, sewer, telephone and electricity. She was happy with her completed hurdles.

The efficient Drum took care of the meetings with City Hall for proper zoning, permits and fees. He was very capable and energetic. He rented space to conduct her business. When the news spread, interested doctors from far away cities, who wanted to relocate, and recently graduated doctors called on her and willingly offered to invest money for a share of profits and a position on the staff.

From her vantage point of observing the candidates, she looked apprehensive as a tall, blonde man approached her. He looked familiar but she wasn't certain she knew him. He stood before her, smiled broadly and asked, "Are you Sophee Tillers?" He seemed happy as he continued, "You have really changed since the last time we played together."

She smiled, "Yes, I am Sophee Tillers." She looked puzzled, "Did we play together on the farm that many years ago?"

"I am disappointed that you have forgotten me. I am Tharpe Gunter, who grew up on the Tillers Estate."

Sophee blushed, "You recognized me without the blubber?"

He laughed, "No. I asked for you and someone pointed you out to me. I would not have recognized you. How did you overcome your painful shyness? And how did you get so thin and gorgeous?"

She smiled and saw the long line advancing, she smiled, "It is really a long and interesting story."

"Let's talk about us later. I am in a hurry but I am here to see about investing in your hospital and becoming one of its pediatricians."

Sophee smiled at him, "I am glad one of the residents from the farm achieved success. That's very nice. I like that very much. Thank you for wanting to practice here. Drum, my attorney, will prepare the legal papers. Call me or come by, I am living in my folks' cottage which has not changed. I'll be home after nine. It's good to see you."

She recalled the painful memories of the obese girl who played with the children on the estate when she was taken by Emily to learn how to get along with children a lifetime ago. She had never learned the secret of getting along. Tharpe looked sad and troubled so perhaps he had never learned or he had forgotten.

Sophee urged Drum to receive all the money but leave her as owner since Tillers Estate could have constructed hospital without assistance but Drum and other advisers insisted on her allowing interested parties to make investments. She had become alarmed at the cost of equipment but she was living an all-time high in using credit. She advertised the job and Tokks Construction and Engineering Company was awarded the bid and subbed out most of the project. Tharpe Gunter was returning to Longbranch at the end of the year and assuming a position on the staff as head of pediatrics.

They had a nice visit the day he was in town to invest but there was no chance of future or promise of future romance between them. He was going through divorce and wanted to start over back home. There were no children but his wife was given the home and a car. He did not want to live in same town with her after having been married fourteen years. Especially since they shared same friendships and too, he still felt love for her.

Sophee ran an ad for hospital administrator in several large newspapers, especially in Claire's hometown. She was hoping to snag Schwinn Swanson. She believed in happy endings for lovers, particularly those who were married. She owed Claire much more than her returning husband. As the hospital neared completion, Schwinn Swanson showed up in answer to Sophee's ad. He looked healthy, sober and alert. Sophee asked, "Are you here in Longbranch for a job or to see your wife, Claire?"

Very calmly he replied, "Both, but I need the job first. She won't give me the time of day if I am not employed. Since you asked your question about her, I assume you know all about me and Claire."

Sophee was elated as she replied, "I know Claire. She is my best friend. So far, you are the only candidate who qualifies, so I guess you can go to work as soon as possible and get our new hospital ready for operation before it is completed. Call Claire, she is in the phone book."

Sophee motioned for Drum who put Schwinn in charge of hiring all personnel and meeting with the board to learn how it would be operated, and learn all the rudiments of administering to the success of Tillers Memorial Medical Center. She worked long hours and met with a hodge podge of politicians, government agencies that had to be appeased, suppliers, dealers, service experts and her banker who was always giving her money to pay out.

She and the mayor arranged ribbon cutting exercises that included lots of publicity. Drum and Schwinn worked well together. Sophee was proud of herself, for Claire and for Schwinn to see how well he handled difficult situations quickly and resolved them before they turned into everlasting and troublesome problems. Several of her classmates from nursing school applied for jobs. She felt they were working for her for once. She felt elated over what her money had created.

She met with representatives of hospital board of Longbranch General. They planned to have overlapping care with Tillers having more specialists to allow all cases to be cared for at home. She walked in a daze and wondered when she would awaken. Claire, Hans, and the other children all supported her and gave her encouragement. Jeremiah congratulated her. "It makes me happy to know of your capabilities, cuz. You are really one of us, after all." He was impressed with her financial acumen in that she was not depleting the till.

Her desire to run haunted her. Fearing she was being driven through internal strife to leave again before her project was completed, Sophee brought a new and larger community center to Longbranch. As long as investors wanted to spend their money, she decided the citizens needed a center that catered to all ages who desired to take advantage of what it offered, especially to senior citizens and a day care center for working mothers that was affordable and to the current trend of the residents in attending concerts. She was giving them culture.

CHAPTER ELEVEN

When Aunt Gerta and Uncle Edward chose to be treated at her hospital instead of the more familiar one, Sophee was shocked but when she received the urgent message that they wanted to see her, she almost went into shock. She left the floor immediately in her uniform and leaning over Aunt Gerta's bed, she heard words that she never dreamed possible. Aunt Gerta asked Sophee, "Will you forgive a foolish and bitter old woman for mistreating you when you had no one to defend you except Emily and Abram? I don't know why I acted as I did but I am sorry for any pain I caused you. Please forgive me and in that forgiveness, will you allow me and Edward to be buried side by side near Hans and Abram? I hope I am not too late in asking this. I have suffered but I was too proud to ask you. I never thought you had enough sense to amount to anything. But you did and I didn't. Please, forgive me now as I lay on my dying bed. Edward is waiting down the hall to say the same things. We have been friends in our old age. We were stupid."

Sophee searched her soul and remembered Netta and Emily who always insisted that forgiveness was His order of expectations. She held Aunt Gerta's hand as she spoke, "I forgive you, and you and Uncle Edward belong near daddy and Uncle Abram. It is sometimes almost impossible to be a mother. One never knows the answers nor the correct decisions to make when there is no one there to guide you. Go in peace and abide in His love in the time you have left. I forgave you long ago so both of us are guilty. Forgive me for not loving you as a child. Thank you for offering peace. Maybe living with myself will now be easier. Goodbye Aunt Gerta. I'll see Uncle Edward now to assure him he can be laid to rest in the plot of his choice."

Sophee observed how old her uncle Edward was. She felt guilty for allowing her hate to eat at her all her life. She leaned over to him, "Uncle Edward, I have just come from seeing Aunt Gerta. I forgive you both for not using sound judgment in your treatment of me as a child. I guess you did something right since I turned out all right."

"Please forgive me Sophee. I knew Gerta was wrong but I was too mean to interfere. I was jealous of you when she gave you any kind of treatment and it pleased me when you were unhappy. I guess we were both sick in turning your care over to Emily, a stranger. You must be a good person to forgive us but I can leave here now more freely, knowing you accepted our plea for forgiveness and hopefully you will bury us in the Tillers' cemetery. We would both appreciate that."

"Uncle Edward, rest in peace. You will be buried beside Aunt Gerta in the Tillers' Cemetery and I shall take as much care in seeing to your graves as I do the others buried there. You were kind enough to take me into your home, so I thank you for that and I forgive you both. I guess you did the best you knew how to do since you never had children of your own. Goodbye Uncle Edward."

Aunt Gerta was first patient to die in the new hospital and Uncle Edward was the second. They were very old and never had close friends who made allowances for their meanness. Sophee buried them near Hans and Abram and their wives. It was a splendid funeral and citizens of the town sent flowers which mattered greatly to Sophee. It was the christian thing for Sophee to do. They had arrived in their adopted country together and deserved to share final resting place together on Tillers land. The three siblings loved one another. The horrible thing for her to know was the truth that she wasn't loved by Aunt Gerta and apparently by her father since he chose to go with his wife rather than live for his daughter who had caused her to be conceived.

Life resumed and Sophee felt relieved that at the end they cared. She enjoyed working as a nurse in pediatrics with Dr. Gunter who loved to reminisce about his time spent on the farm but he did not mention that his parents were still there since they owned their home. Sophee decided to keep his parents informed of their son's progress. She dropped by occasionally for short visits and was always surprised at the gracious manner she was always received. She derived great joy from the visits.

She did not love the land because she could not feel its love and what it represented. Consequently she felt no love, not even self love. Her secret was never revealed that she hoped to share love at least once in her life. She felt guilty for not feeling great love for Hans who poured out his love to Claire and Schwinn. Claire and Schwinn were honeymooning after being separated for many years. The children accepted him as their father, even Hans, who was as love-starved as she. Sophee felt left out so to spare her wounded feelings she didn't visit as often as before. They in turn didn't visit her. She didn't know which was worse, to stay away and hurt and miss not seeing them or visit, see them and feel rejected and rush home to cry. She did not want to run again but she felt the intense desire to hit the road and learn why she always ran. She lacked the courage to stand and fight the unseen enemy. She usually left without notice, idled away her time, wallowed in guilt and self pity and returned, only to escape again when she could not cope with pressures she encountered while living.

To anchor her to her responsibilities as a Tillers, and to the people who depended on her in Longbranch, Sophee decided to choose a section of land like her dwellers and to build her a house and make it a home on choice three hundred and fifty acres and try farming and nursing. Needing an unbiased decision, she contacted Drum at work, "Since you are single and probably in the market for a house and land and also someone I admire and appreciate the expedient manner in which you get things done and the way you think. You are fast on your feet and very observant. Will you help me select a farm free standing land for sale or from the land on the Tillers Estate. I want the best acreage possible. Help me choose best site for my new home. I have lived in my parents' home long enough. You are only single male who can give an honest answer. Especially since we brought the perfect hospital to town. Will you help me?"

He laughed at her suggestion, "Sophee, you know you can't farm. Farming takes more than spending money."

His laughter infuriated her, "I'll become some kind since I want my own land to tend. I guess I could become a pond fisherman."

He looked at her from top to bottom and from bottom to top and as he licked his lips, he replied," I'll help you if you will go with me to the country club dance Saturday night."

She stood to leave as she shouted, "Sorry, I can't do that. I don't dance. Thanks for nothing anyway."

He followed her out of the office and shouted, "I thought you could do just about everything and were not the type to resort to saying no by using excuses."

She hept on walking, realizing Drum had misunderstood her friendly help. He thought she was advertising but he had nothing for sale. She was furious so she chose to ride out to the home of the couple who had managed her vast personal acreage to get his opinion. He, his wife, and Sophee drove over the land in his truck. He pointed out advantages and disadvantages. Malcolm Petrie slowed the truck after driving through a dense grove of large oak trees. As he approached a clearing with a smooth grass covered area and domestic flowers growing wild at the edges and blooming and unpruned shrubbery some of which Sophee recognized, he explained as he stopped his truck, "This land is not for sale. It is tied up in litigation in the courts. It is reported that this was one of the original sites where the first settlers built their homes. It looks like the house vanished since there are no chimneys standing nor any debris that resembles brick. I like to lean against the old graceful oaks and reminisce about life here way back then. Can't you hear the children's laughter and the music all about us? There is a small stream that runs a few hundred yards from here. The only disturbance showing that someone once lived here is the old well now filled with trash and debris."

Monique sighed, "Too bad we can't locate the owner or the person who represents the owner. You would enjoy building your home in this clearing and watch and enjoy your stately trees. A two or three story house is necessary for you to appreciate them. I can feel the vibrations that this land wants to give happiness of ownership to someone."

Malcolm said in a pensive manner, "If you are interested in buying this land, we must begin at city hall. It has more than the acres you said you wanted. Shall we begin?"

Sophee spread out her arms as if enveloping the land, said, "I'll call Jeremiah in the morning to have him search the legal side of why it can't be bought.

Malcolm, call the surveyor we always use and have him standing by for quick service. With prayer, perhaps I can have the deed in my hands before sundown by next Friday. It may be more land than I wanted but I can't hesitate. After all, I can afford it."

They laughed as Malcolm spoke, "Do you have any suggestions about the kind of house that should be built here since you would be my neighbor? It will be shocking to poor Jeremiah and Jason to learn that you possess strange tendencies to settle down, live and work here on the land. We better proceed slowly with caution since you will be putting them in shock. Your Uncle Abram always said you would return to the land since you are your father's daughter with the pride of farming instilled in you. You have dodged the issue long enough."

Sophee smiled, "Yes, I have. It is time, isn't it? Do you and Monique have any preference for a place that you seem to love so much? What does the land deserve?

Malcolm rubbed his hand along the side of his face and began, "Well, there is a well known artist who visits here when the weather is good. He parks his home and takes out his easel and makes the trees come to life on the canvas. He is a hermit but shops in Longbranch and loves Monique's southern cooking. He showed me the blueprints of the house he says belongs here. I agree with him. It suits the terrain. He keeps changing the design so he can make it the way nature intended to have it. He doesn't take too kindly to strangers, especially females. He is harmless though and a perfect gentleman. I'll contact you after we find out if you can buy the land and after he agrees to show you his house plans."

"Thank you Malcolm. This is your favorite place, isn't it? Could you give it up?"

"We never owned it. We only had our dreams but there is some land I have been looking at and if you want to sign for me, I can buy it and take care of both our farms. My dreams don't always come true but to you, we could give up this land. We love you and want you to live among us. You have given us security and provided homes that the majority of us could not have bought. We owe you a lot and are looking forward to the day you can make this land yours and can decide that the land is what you want and need. This is what you need to satisfy your soul to cease your running. We could build you a house in no time. This is heaven to us. Monique and I walk through the woods on our way down to the stream when we go fishing. The symmetry of the huge limbs and how they entwine and stand so strong throughout the heavy winds consoles us and grants us peace and renewed strength. We lovingly refer to it as Eden. We feel like we have been welcomed for a brief visit. Sometimes we feel we are being watched but in a safe manner. It is like a home to us, you know, the invisible one. It is our favorite place to relax."

Sophee raised her voice, "Please don't go on when there is no way for me to own it."

Monique smiled, "Nothing helps like prayer. Since you would not cut the trees and strip or damage the land, the land will work for you to get it. It suits you. We always wanted to share it with someone who loves it as we always have. You have never lived "at home" so now the land will become yours to love and live forever."

Sophee began to cry, "Monique, that is my secret. I am anxious to leave again which scares me. I have been cheated, all that I own and no one to share it with me. I want something to anchor me here since I leave but always come back. Why keep leaving? The land is the reason I want to hold me. I am so alone. Noah certainly would have turned me aside since all his passengers went aboard two by two. I truly want what everyone else at Tillers has even if it means working for me. Do you two ever feel like crying when you visit this little piece of America that grants one so many intangible quantities of beauty?"

Monique and Malcome nodded and smiled as Monique spoke, "I cry every time we spend a few minutes here at the clearing where nothing has ever grown except a thick blanket of grass and a few flowers along the edge of the clearing. I think this is your destined home where you will finally plant your roots and settle down until the end among folks who know and love you."

Sophee wrapped her arms around Monique, "I hope so, Monique. If I get a chance I'll give it my best effort."

They drove back to the Petrie home and as Sophee walked to her car, she said, "Thank you both for allowing me to attempt to realize my dream without casting me aside since I know nothing about the operation of a farm and the rudiments of planning year after year. I have never seen that clearing before so I plan to investigate and hopefully claim it as mine. If I had it, giving it up, I know, would be like having the last child to leave home enduring an emptiness that can't be filled. I appreciate your sharing it with me. When I buy it, we will share and we will make the kind of home the original owners would accept since I feel they will communicate with us if they are not satisfied. We shall enter into this together to make us happy. I am looking forward to seeing the house your friend designed. We must include him in its construction if he is around since he loves this spot as much as we do. Goodnight. Call if you hear anything that is in my favor. I am home until two every day now since I work the second shift at the hospital."

In accepting Malcom's dinner invitation, she realized she was accepting a leap toward loving her land, at least become a part of her heritage. There had been no news from Jeremiah's investigation but all of them were hoping. Koa Declah, a self-styled recluse and hermit, had agreed to show Sophee his house plans. She knew nothing about him and Malcolm claimed he knew nothing so exercising her gambler's rights, she was having dinner with him and the Petrie's as something of a blind date. Arriving home from first shift that she had exchanged with a co-worker, Sophee called Claire to exchange her daily report and then rushed to arrive at Malcom and Monique's before Koa arrived. He evidently had the same thought since his van was parked in the yard.

Faced with no other alternative, she walked across the porch and knocked. She was very nervous but entered calmly as soon as Malcolm invited her. Malcolm took charge. It was his home and being a gentleman, he acted as host. He sensed Sophee's hesitancy and feeling sorry for her without letting her know, he placed his hand on her arm, "Koa Declah, I would like for you to meet Sophee Tillers, my dear friend. Sophee, meet Koa, the artist."

Sophee smiled at the big, rugged man, with long brown hair and heavy beard with penetrating grey eyes and a no-nonsense smile that revealed a perfect alignment of large pearly white teeth. He extended his hand and when she placed her hand in his, he placed his other hand over hers. He smiled and looked at her, "Miss Tillers, we finally meet. It is a pleasure. I have waited a long time to see you in person."

Sophee looked at him and smiled as she asked, "Have I been in your presence or was I supposed to meet you?"

He smiled, "Your host and hostess have talked of you during the time I have known them. They have always wanted us to meet. Malcolm refers to us as non-sociable hermits in need of change."

Sophee relaxed as she smiled and turned toward her host and hostess, Malcolm and Monique who were smiling. She said, "Malcolm, Monique, you romantic matchmakers. At last Koa and I make you happy."

Malcolm asked, "Could I offer you something to drink."

Koa smiled and quickly replied, "I am sure Monique has her well planned dinner ready so nothing for me, thanks."

"Thanks Malcolm, but nothing for me either."

Their eyes met briefly as if in understanding. Sophee wanted to shout that she was still celebrating birthdays but thought perhaps all dwellers on Tillers Estate knew all about the wild escapades of its eccentric owner and Koa need not be informed. She had always been pampered and spoiled by her Uncle and persecuted by her Aunt and perhaps deserted by her father and bereft of her mother in death. It angered her that she was not her person but theirs.

Koa asked, "Sophee, are you serious about claiming my place of solitude to build your permanent home?"

"Yes, if only I can buy it. I understand that you have the perfectly designed home in mind for it."

He smiled at her anxiety, "Since the first time I found it. The spot seems to dominate my thoughts."

Sophee asked, "Could I see your plans?"

He smiled, "Patience my dear. After dinner, yes, and then one day before you decide to build, I 'd like to walk over the area with you to get a true sense of how you think the house should be built. I hope to pick up on vibrations that are present if it is prudent for you to live there. But tonight we eat and get to know what each one wants in the house. If you have never eaten Monique's superb cooking, you are in for a treat."

Monique served a scrumptious dinner of baked chicken with lots of spices, green bean casserole, stewed corn, fried okra, sliced tomatoes fresh from her garden, home made bisuits, iced tea and peach cobbler for dessert. Everyone was quiet as they feasted.

Sophee asked over dessert, "Koa, where do you call home?"

He smiled at her, "In my van on the roads and by-ways, wherever I may decide to roam."

She almost laughed at his evasion, "Well, where do you pay your taxes?"

He laughed, "A bit persistent, I see. Wherever I am living at the time I am told my taxes are due in order to remain. I am a world traveler without a home to keep while I am on the road. I grow stale after I have been too long in one place. Do you like to travel, Sophee?"

Malcolm answered quickly, "She doesn't like to stay home since she is always off again too soon after being here for awhile. This is the longest time she has stayed put. She is not like me. I like to put my feet under my table every day and sleep in my bed with my head on my pillow in the same place every night with my beloved wife always beside me."

Sophee laughed, "When I feel the urge to run, I just go, but I always return for awhile and then leave again, never with destination in my mind. I have to get away. I don't know why though. That is why I want a home and my own land to yield a profit, hopefully at farming and tilling the land. I haven't decided on that yet but I need a yoke or an anchor to weigh me down and hold me here."

Koa asked, "Have you tried marriage? That's supposed to be a perfect yoke."

Sophee was getting serious, "Yes. I have tried it twice and failed twice. You are right, it is a perfect yoke if I could remain married for longer than I was married. I broke the record both times in getting quick divorces."

Malcolm wiped his mouth with his napkin as he interrupted, "Tillers Estate could be an excellent yoke but she delegates the operation."

Sophee looked at him and tried to be serious, "Malcolm, for that suggestion, you can help wash the dishes," said Sophee as she leered at him. Malcolm and Sophee had grown up together and after completing college, he had claimed his ten acres for his home while managing her three thousand acres her father had kept for her including the land on which her cottage was located. He later married Monique but had never had any children. He successfully grazed large herds of cattle on most of the land and raised feed for his cattle. He grew tobacco and cotton which required many laborers. In spite of her position, Sophee, Malcolm and Monique were still close friends. He provided her with a horse to exercise and visit the tenants since seeing her among them was all they needed to make them happy. They asked her to park her motorcycle since it was not safe for her. Her presence made their future safe and secure at Tillers as long as she was there to guarantee Tillers' continued operation.

Sophee spoke, "Malcolm, Tharpe Gunter, who is now a pediatrician, is on the staff at Tillers Center. He is settling in town. He is a very good doctor and is getting many new patients. He is also presently surviving a divorce. I am sure he would appreciate a call or a visit from an old friend."

Malcolm looked at her and nodded, "He always operated on all the injured animals. I thought he might become a veterinarian or a surgeon, not a baby doctor. I am glad he made it as a doctor. I will call him but he has kept away from all his sharecropper friends. He was always a bit of a snob."

Koa spoke, "I take it Dr. Gunter grew up with you two here."

Malcolm nodded, "Yes. His parents are still here and are very good farmers. His brother and sister left when they got grown but I don't know where they settled."

Koa looked at Sophee with his piercing grey eyes and asked, "Owning almost the whole county doesn't impress you? You should be aloof, separate and apart, not so available and not one of the working force. You are an enigma. I would estimate that you are also a loyal friend and very selective."

Sophee raised her brow, "Yes, I value my friends. I only have a few but that is my fault, not any other person's fault. I don't make friends very easily. I don't allow them inside to suggest any improvement. I am I. Let's take the heat off me and help Malcolm wash dishes."

Koa smiled. He recognized her dodge in revealing another side of her personality.

Monique said, "We can see the house plans sooner if all of us work together."

The others thought it a good idea and began clearing the table. As Koa unrolled the sheet of the drawing, the three anxious people were quietly watching, thinking he was taking his good slow time in satisfying their peaked curiosity. He used fruit from the bowl that had been removed as the centerpiece and weighted down the edges of the drawing. No one uttered a word. Koa had sketched the trees making them part of the drawing. It was a large two story white frame with four huge columns in front and a porch wrapping itself around front and sides of the house. There was a large terrace off the master bedroom upstairs. Koa explained, "To view the trees through sun and moonlight is purpose of terrace. You and your husband can have your meals served there whenever you like."

Malcolm looked at Sophee in disbelief, knowing how she felt about marriage and sharing her life and home with a man. He awaited the reaction. Sophee looked at Koa in humorous amazement as she said, "I wanted to see your designs of the house not hear your designs of my future. There will be no husband. I like the idea of the terrace and quiet solitude and coffee would be enjoyed there, not served there."

Koa stared at her in horror to think she had rejected his dream. He spoke, "The house demands love and happiness to be shared there and for you to display your wealth by staffing servants to wait on you."

Sophee looked a bit afraid and almost angry as she asked, "Are you saying that I can't use your plans unless I have a husband to move there with me and have many servants?"

Koa was shocked by her action as he spoke, "That is how it is. Without love and marriage, my plans cannot be utilized."

Sophee turned ashen, "Mr. Declah, I am happy the land is not for sale. Your suggestion is highly inappropriate. Malcolm, Monique, the dinner was delicious and up until now the evening was quite nice. Thank you for inviting me. I'll get in touch with you when I find my land. Koa, find your couple to share your dream house but leave me out of it. Your idea is ridiculous. Good night."

The unwanted and uncontrollable flood of tears nearly blinded her but she drove carefully over the familiar roads to her cottage. Her haven of rest which granted her peace and contentment and a place to be alone. She could not understand why she was crying. Was it Koa? It couldn't be. She had only met him one time and once was enough. Was it his blatant charge his precious house was only for married people in love? No. Marriage was a proper institution, nothing new there and he was entitled to his own opinion. Was it her trip down memory lane to dare to become what Uncle Abram wanted her to be? No. Was it her intense desire to run, complicated by spark ignited upon first sight of Koa? Yes. Was she afraid of growing old without ever having love? Yes. She knew he could become her permanent yoke and although she yearned for love, she wasn't prepared to accept his brutal inference. He could mold her into any image he chose. She was rebelling. He seemed as strong as the hold her heritage had on her, a fact she had long ago accepted.

She kept her personal war to herself, finally attempting to confide in Tharpe after Board Meeting where she sat as owner. He asked, "Sophee, you look as unhappy as I feel. Surely you aren't suffering through pangs of divorce, are you?"

Sophee nearly laughed, "Tharpe, it has been too long for me to be suffering over divorce. I am not succeeding in taking advice of my counselor. I need a friend to replace her. Could you possibly be my friend?"

He looked concerned as he asked, "Who is your counselor? Perhaps she is not qualified?"

Sophee looked at his serious face and laughed at his concerned tone. She explained. "I am my own adviser. I don't think I am looking beyond the facts since I recognize my desires and my weaknesses. I need to fire me since I feel I want to give me what I have never wanted but I can't suggest how to improve the situation."

Tharpe suggested, "Since we both need new counselors to start over, have dinner with me tonight and together perhaps we can come up with some workable solution for both of us. Could you meet me at eight at the "Survivors Only" club?"

"Thank you Tharpe. That gets me out of my jail cell and I think I can find the club. I refuse to cry another tear. Until then, so long. I have a shift to complete, but first I have to shed this severe suit of armor and slip into my working uniform. It's rather strange but blissful to fill two pairs of shoes of owner and employee, but I love doing both and no one is complaining. I sometimes appreciate what my old man left me. It gives me power."

He smiled as they headed toward Pediatrics. He leaned toward her and in a very low voice, said, "If I had your money, and your assets, I would not have a problem I could not solve. I would never stay in one place long enough for dust to settle on my money."

"I puzzle many people. I am normally content but something unforeseen and unplanned has suddenly become an irritating force. I am not coping too well and I don't like what it tempts me to do. See you at eight."

"Sophee, the only problems you could possibly have are those you create."

"Perhaps. Perhaps not."

To improve her mental anguish, Sophee rushed by "Maud's Dress Shop" and quickly selected a fancy green dress and a black silk shirtwaist and new accessories. She was boosting her morale to prevent Tharpe's drowning in her sorrow. When she entered the lobby in her new black, he was waiting for her in his black suit, white shirt and black and white striped tie. He looked very suave and debonair and more handsome than he did in his lab coat in which she saw him daily. They were seated in a quiet corner but not far enough from the band. It was not the atmosphere to talk over problem since the diners at nearby tables could hear their necessary shouts. They lingered over dinner and listened to the band and watched the couples having fun while dancing and while shouting, they learned that neither knew how to dance.

In the parking lot, Sophee suggested, "Since neither is attached and neither knows how to dance, why don't we let learning how to dance eliminate our advisers until we can think of another scheme?"

Tharpe smiled at her and said, "My wife always reminded me how dull I was since I couldn't dance and would not try to learn. It's past time for both of us. She now has her own dance partner who also loves her. I am on call

Wednesdays so sign us up for ballroom dancing and the waltz on any other night. If we like it, we can learn the rhumba and shag and win large dance contests."

Sophee smiled, "Learning to dance does sound exciting. It will also make us feel much younger. Thank you for a lovely evening. We will have something to grasp besides our sanity."

After calling several dance studios, Sophee was amazed to learn that all dance studios had full classes and large waiting lists. She grew rather smugly that they were not alone in not knowing the basics of life so many took for granted. She felt relieved that others did not know how either. After finding one with the shortest waiting period, Sophee rushed to "Jackie's Tap Tap", a dance studio that offered more than tap dancing and signed them up for the next two sessions. She chose to have lessons twice weekly to expedite therapy and extend fun time. Tharpe accepted her proposal with excitement.

To while away their theraputic time, Tharpe agreed to accompany Sophee to dinner at Claire's. She failed to tell him she was exposing him to family life by not informing him of the dozen children and a sitter, Tosca. Exposing him to what having children meant, she chose the shock treatment of exposure. To experiment further, she insisted on him picking her up at the "big boss lady's" cottage. He displayed no outward emotion other than being very tense.

Before Sophee's knock at the front door, Hans opened the door and hugged her and without a welcome, rushed them toward the activity room where everyone was watching end of children's special television show. Schwinn greeted them and resumed watching until show was over. Sophee laughed to think she and Tharpe weren't guests, just part of the family.

After the last child had left the room, Tharpe and Sophee were invited into dining room. When Tharpe saw the number of places set at the table, he turned to Sophee and smiled, but when he observed the two large platters of fried chicken, he patted her on the shoulder. He explored the table further, knowing the shocks were over, but to see two large bowls of potato salad, two large bowls of tiny green butter beans, two large stacks of yellow corn on the cob, several baskets of homemade biscuits and many glasses of milk, he was happy to see the house was filled with love and care. He smiled at Sophee as she grinned at his exhuberance by witnessing love at its finest. He stood and watched children of all sizes and ages gathering for the evening meal. When all were present, they joined hands and said grace together while being led by Claire, "Bless this bounty that You have provided and bless each of us here who labor under Your love and guidance, Amen." All echoed amens and Sophee witnessed happiness shining on Tharpe's face. Sophee smiled at him. He confessed later that he found something he had missed.

When food was passed, Tharpe became a kid again and quickly served his plate. He knew seconds were not guaranteed. Total silence was observed until Tharpe heard, "Please pass the chicken,". "Pass it to me after you get served, please." "Pass the biscuits, please." "Yes, pass them around, please." "Pass the corn and the butter, please." "I need another napkin, please." "Me, too." "Someone please pass the salad." "Yeah, pass it on down to me." "Anna Marie, don't hog the beans, pass them around again, please." "Mama, could I have another napkin, please." The many voices pleased Tharpe and Sophee. "Pour me some more milk, please." "When are you bringing in the cake, mama?"

Tosca and Claire pushed their chairs from the table. Claire soon returned with a birthday cake on which were four lighted candles. Claire placed the cake in front of Tharpe as Sophee quickly removed his empty plate and set it in hers. Tosca stopped at end of table with ice cream and dishes. Tharpe looked at Sophee as he read the blue and green lettering, "Happy birthday, Doctor Gunter." He smiled at Claire and the voices chipped in, "Make a wish, quick and blow out your candles. You have to be told what to do like us, since you are only four years old." He smiled at them and there were many happy giggles. As he blew out the candles, Sophee saw moisture in his eyes. Everyone sang happy birthday and the children yelled, "Speech! Speech!"

Tharpe smiled at them and said, "If someone will give me a knife, I'll serve all of you a generous slice of cake to go with the ice cream I see at the end of the table where Tosca is busily filling bowls."

Tharpe smiled as he heard, "Ole! Ole!"

Schwinn smiled at Tharpe as he retrieved from the buffet a specially wrapped gift and placed it in front of him, "Happy birthday from all of us."

Tharpe opened it slowly and carefully and when he saw the cassette tape he had been looking for, he looked at Schwinn, smiled and said, "I wondered why you wanted to know what kind of music I preferred. Thank all of you very much, for the birthday dinner, cake and present. Let's enjoy the tape after we share this delightful cake I am certain Claire and you children baked."

The children read, "Otto at the Keyboard" on the label and when they heard the beautiful piano melodies, the children listened with great interest, totally enraptured. When the final note was heard, there was a tremendous applause, and then, "Daddy, you bought that tape to urge us to practice." "I wonder how long he had to practice to learn to play like that." "Man, he's great." "What a touch!" "Thank you Doc for sharing that with us." "This has been the best birthday party ever." "Thanks for having Doc's birthday here mother Sophee, it gives us a reason to stay up beyond our scheduled bedtime. Goodnight mother Sophee, goodnight Doctor Gunter, goodnight Mama, goodnight Daddy, goodnight Tosca, and goodnight all."

Each child hugged Sophee and shook Tharpe's hand and kissed Claire and Schwinn and waved to Tosca as they marched off to bed with tiny Tabatha toddling along with them. Tosca, Claire and Sophee cleaned up dining room and washed the dishes, after which Tosca joined the children as Claire and Sophee carried after dinner coffee into activity room to join Schwinn and Tharpe.

Everyone seemed totally relaxed as Schwinn brought up problem to Sophee about place for nurses to live since the single nurses did not have cars and could not afford a car and an apartment in town. She asked Schwinn to contact Jeremiah about converting Aunt Gerta's house and adding rooms to serve as their dorm and to hire housemothers to see that they were properly cared for and supervised to satisfy their parents, guardians or relatives. She explained they could ride city bus since bus ran every hour.

In shocked amazement Tharpe asked, "Sophee, had you made that decision before he asked the question?"

Sophee quickly answered, "Schwinn and I hold hospital meetings whenever we are together. Aunt Gerta and Uncle Edward died recently. I own their house and I need to do something with it. I don't need it to live in and since it is furnished and empty, I am glad I have a need for it. Why do you ask?"

He crossed his legs, "I thought you made a rapid decision without thinking of the consequences. I admire you in getting things done but I suppose you have had heavy responsibilities for a very long time and I suppose it is easy for you. I can't make important decisions like you. We must be leaving since we are both on the early shift. I think seven comes much earlier than it did when I was younger. Just think, four at last." He turned to Claire, "I dare not ask how you knew it was my birthday, I think I know. Thank you very much. Do I have to wait for invitations from Sophee to visit again?"

Schwinn said, "Come anytime but come especially during lambing season and shearing time. We will let you earn your grub. Just drop by, someone is always home. Treat our home as yours."

Tharpe seemed to relax as he replied, "You don't know what you are saying. I will possibly make a nuisance of myself. Bring the children in for a free first time exam. I didn't know such wonderful people still lived in Longbranch. It restores my faith in mankind. Perhaps Sophee's assistance is helping me drop my guard. Goodnight and thanks again. You have a wonderful family. I wish you continued happiness."

Sophee explained to Tharpe about Claire's adopted family and all about Hans being hers but not about why he lived with Claire.

While waiting for dance classes to begin, Sophee took him to dinner at Jeremiah and Latrelles and Jason's. Surprisingly, Jason's friend, Sara Tshinsky, was his guest. Tharpe was impressed with large oval frames that held pictures of Doyle and Juanita Hepstart, Gerta and Edward Green, Hans and Lutricia Tillers, Abram and Merle Tillers, Audrey and Pierce Molens, and Clothilda and Grieg Tillers, Sophee's relatives. There was a picture of the beach house and the river house. Latrelle had adopted the position as historian and collected what pictures she could and Sophee had given her all the pictures she could find and an excellent photo album was on display in the den. On another wall were modern brass frames of Jeremiah and Latrelle, Jason, Sophee and Hans, Ned and Jackie

Shearouse, Merle's parents and Tom and Laura Lumax, Latrelle's parents and Lloyd and Patience Snellen, Merle's grand parents. There were large pictures of Claire, Schwinn and children with Hans. The picture of Emily Jackson and Netta Jelks also puzzled Tharpe. He decided to admire family portraits and ask Sophee questions when they were alone. He was seeing integral part of Sophee's life that added to her greatness of which she was not aware. Tharpe became uneasy as he thought Sophee's family could be thinking of finding her a mate. He shrugged.

CHAPTER TWELVE

Even in the presence of Tharpe, Sophee still thought of Koa but she had written him off since he had not contacted her. She wanted to take Tharpe to see Malcolm and Monique but was afraid Koa's name would be mentioned or that he would be their guest. She accepted her silly actions as a childish tantrum. She made arrangements to have dinner with Tharpe's parents, to which he objected but went with her when she convinced him it was the proper thing for a successful doctor to do and it behooved him to call on them as their son. His folks were very proud of him and the evening was trying even after a delightful dinner of baked ham, candied yams, turnips, apple sauce, cornbread and butter and all the victuals of a southern country dinner. Mrs. Gunter showed Tharpe pictures of his brother, Lucious and his sister, Kathleen. They visited recently after having been gone for over five years. Tharpe promised to bring or send them pictures of him as he and Sophee were leaving.

Knowing how Tharpe felt about his sharecropper heritage, Sophee decided to make his parents happy by sending his pictures to them. She began taking pictures of him at work, near his car, visiting Claire and family and other candid shots. She took the pictures to his parents with the explanation that she knew Tharpe was too busy to get them out to them.

Mrs. Gunter smiled through her tears and touched Sophee's arm, "He is a proud man and resents having sharecroppers for parents. I am quite surprised he is allowed to be seen with you. He has always referred to you as "big boss lady" but the sharecroppers put him through medical school, thanks to you. He needs to know his true origin."

Sophee smiled at the troubled lady and explained, "He is suffering greatly. He did not want the divorce. He wanted children and he is still in love with his wife. My services are more rewarding and friendlier in helping him adjust to single life than hiring a psychiatrist or a shrink. I am his theraputic adviser, nothing more. I know his pet name for me and that is all right. As soon as he learns to cope, our being together will no longer be necessary."

Mrs. Gunter seemed surprised by Sophee's candor as she replied, "Thank you for telling me that. Do you know why he chose to return to Longbranch since he feels as he has always felt? That a son of a sharecropper was the worst thing in the world to have to be?"

Sophee hugged her, "He is unconsciously returning to his roots. Don't give up on him, yet. He might become your son again after all this adjustment is over. Since he works at the hospital, he must be planning to remain in town. You will probably have your son sooner than you think."

"Thank you for the pictures and your faith in our son. You are the kindest person I have ever known. Go with God's blessing."

All in the name of therapy, Sophee pulled Tharpe in their formal attire to hear the City Symphony. He seemed happier after she took him to the concert at the new Tillers Center, and to the church to hear special contata, and finally to school to see Claire's children perform in school play. He was responding to prescribed therapy slowly but Sophee was proud to see the expected adjustment.

They endured the awkward beginning of becoming graceful dancers and the close contact never bothered them. At the end of sessions, Tharpe was adjusting to single life and learning to live with endurable hurt. Neither had discussed Sophee's problem. Nothing had changed in her life. She was still not the center of anyone's life and in her position she had no insurmountable odds to overcome. Money could buy her anything. She did not despair and knew her services as Tharpe's adviser were over when he curtailed spending time with her when they had no prescribed therapy. His spare time was spent at Claire's and his parents. He yearned for children and enjoyed what Claire's represented. Soon Sophee saw him at work only. She felt guilt at being with handsome and eligible doctor without feeling an iota of romantic response. One day she still hoped to feel and to have feeling returned. Koa's face appeared in her thoughts but only for a second.

The happy times she had spent with Malcolm and Monique were theirs and Koa's name was never mentioned. Jeremiah had succeeded in contacting all the owners of her dream land and was optimistic that all were on the edge of selling since no one before her had pursued them with such determination. They requested a conference with her and Jeremiah assured her that was a good sign.

When Sophee and Jeremiah entered the other attorney's office, they were faced with five stone-faced women and one happy man. One woman did not wait for the attorneys to conduct the meeting. She asked immediately what Sophee's plans were for their land. Sophee smiled at her and explained, "That certain spot demonstrates what America really is like, beautiful and purposeful. I wish to build my home in the clearing and farm the land and perhaps raise cattle on the excellent grass found there."

The woman leaned toward Sophee as she asked, "Are you married?"

Sophee looked searchingly into her eyes and responded, "No, ma'am but it is because I do not wish to be married. I am capable and am financially solvent enough to make the land fulfill its purpose for which its original owners intended. If I choose to marry, the man must also be of the land and willing to carry on and protect it from investors who might want to blemish its beauty, especially mar the trees and deface the lovely gardens. I admire it and wish to let it remain as close to its original beauty as possible. You will be pleased with the plans I have for the land. I feel that you love it as much as I do and I only recently found it."

They looked at each other and nothing was said, then the happy man said, "Well, ladies, I think we have found logical buyer. She sounds like ma, the way she feels about the old place. I agree to sell. What about the rest of you?"

They agreed and surprisingly they seemed relieved. The one who had spoken said, "We feel you will find as much happiness in owning it as all the people who owned it before us. The old home place burned and the chimneys were torn down and used to build another house on a smaller lot. We love the trees and we will visit them to see how long they'll last. We will not disturb you. Enjoy the land. It is yours to live on and be happy. We will sign over the land today. I guess the rest will be left to our lawyers. Thank you for seeing us. Good bye dear. You seem so young."

After surveying and recording the deed, Jeremiah made a special trip to tell Sophee. He assured her she could build on her property at any time. He blushed as she kissed him and thanked him for his excellent work. She said, "Send me a bill for your services, dear cousin. This is one that I will enjoy paying. I wish Uncle Abram were here to witness my inclinations towards settling on the land. I really tried his patience but we truly shared a great love. I have often felt I owed him my very life and existence. If I keep this up, I am certain to cry so thank you and I again thank you for getting me what I really wanted more than anything right now. See you."

Jeremiah left laughing and said, "How long will this please you and keep you settled on the land?"

Sophee raised her voice to his departing back, "Who knows? This might be the yoke that chokes me. I get so tired of running. Until you have experienced that terrible drive, you cannot understand. I know I entertain people with my conduct but that's the way I am and I get completely out of control if I don't satisfy that yearning. Only to return and repeat the performance. I'll retire here since the monthly payments are so huge. I think you deliberately did that to hold me here. Get away from here!"

While waiting for Koa to return and build his house on her spot of paradise, she and Malcolm selected the perfect spot beside the stream for Sophee to erect a temporary cabin. After many conflicting decisions after looking at so many designs, she bought blueprints for two-story cabin with attached enclosed carport or garage, to be built near stream but still in edge of the woods. It was simple in design. Downstairs were large kitchen, dining room and living room with bar as partition, pantry and storage room, full bath, and laundry room all enclosed. Two tiers of steps led upstairs to one large bedroom and one small bedroom with hall and doors that opened onto porch. She was proudest of her walk-in closet and large bath. A screened in porch upstairs and downstairs were added by her. She wanted to observe the beauty around her, and no one would disturb her since private entrances granted total privacy. Entrance by invitation only, and where Sophee decided to spend most of her spare time since she could view the stream and the trees in each direction and watch the magic of congregating birds and the silent and softly flowing water that glittered in the early morning sunlight.

71

Malcolm and Drum, who had fallen in love and acted like any other sensible young man, hired crews to extend electricity, telephone service and have light pole erected. In rapid time septic tank was installed. The last assignment was having a well dug with electric pump installed to guarantee indoor plumbing. To exert her authority, she had a miniature copy of the cabin built as a pump house to protect it from freezing in the harsh winters. She was amazed in learning that there were so many ramifications to building and supplying construction with necessary comforts. She laughed as she learned but kept her ignorance to herself.

While her cabin was getting underway, Tharpe called her to explain his poor manners. He began, "I know you think me heartless for not saying thanks for readjudicating me—but now I can say it. I have a few hangups that distort my true feelings but through your expertise as counselor, I have made up with my parents. Thanks for covering my butt by sending them pictures I had promised. They love you, but they always have. The dejected feelings my divorce caused and the love I had for my wife are all resolved and final. I am now looking for love. You are superb. I wish I had your strength to live alone and love it. I have been dating a doctor from Longbranch General. I am not in love but it is a beginning. She is also divorced with two boys. I feel you made my problems yours and helped me adjust. However, I feel like a heel since I never once asked you about your problem. I am having fun again and my life now has direction. Have you resolved your problems by helping me?"

She wanted to lecture but knew its futility, so she answered, "It resolved itself so things are working right for a change. I am happy for you. If you ever need a friend, call."

"Thanks for giving me Claire, Schwinn and their family. Sharing their happiness is great therapy for me. I haven't been this happy in years. Take care. See you at work."

Sophee wanted to reply, "Big boss lady is still big boss lady."

Sophee broke her promise to herself by losing control. She cried when first scoop of dirt was dug for foundation of her cabin, her second creation besides Hans. She was finally building something of her own and something to leave on earth signifying to others who investigated records that she had actually been here. Her large estate was hers to carve into everlasting image of Sophee, the woman. She would settle for her many acres over the ten Tillers acres that she had originally bargained for to tend the three hundred fifty acres as her other dwellers of the estate but fate had intervened and she now was in process of buying her land to share with whomever she pleased.

She had endured life at Aunt Gerta's, in dinky apartments, hospital wards, dorms, tents and her parents' cottage and had not suffered too greatly. Now she would live in what she was building and rule as queen to give her all the things she could buy. It was a chore to select everything but she knew she could do it because she wanted to please herself. She could give herself the best if no one wanted to share her life; she would spend her life and love on material things.

The design of kitchen cabinets and bookcases in bedrooms and countertops was hers and blending floor color and design of tile was her choice. Even the small downstairs bathroom needed choice of fixtures, walls and floor covering. Every day between three and time stores closed, Sophee was collecting samples for something and she was still on first floor. She was spared many decisions; she only requested concrete slab and sealant for two car garage. It seemed her crew worked too fast to be doing job correctly but she kept up mad pace to have material and supplies ready for them to prevent any delays.

Malcolm exercised great patience in having samples returned if they were not what was needed or if they did not please her. They were pleased with her fastest decision which was for her stove, refrigerator, freezer, dishwasher, garbage disposal, washer and dryer, hot water heater and heat pump. The crew had designed only one place for them to fit and only one color to decide upon since all walls were white, so she could not change her mind. Her decision to paint the kitchen wall white was that the morning sun made her cabin very bright and the white appliances pleased her. She chose many colors for walls but settled on white throughout the cabin and stood by her decision. Her chosen tile for her kitchen and bath and dining area and enclosed rooms was one of multi colored pastel specks on white squares and same color of carpet for living room. She chose abstract blue and white shelf paper for her kitchen cabinets and shelves of her pantry and laundry room. Picking up blue in tile for her couch and chairs she chose a lovely shade of blue and as a concession to nonexistent friends, she bought a love seat daybed to sleep one extra guest. Her dinette suit was blonde wood and glass, with table, eight chairs and china cabinet. She chose same style tables for living room. She installed ivory blinds and thick white sheers for living room and blue cotton curtains with white abstract designs for kitchen. She carpeted the steps and the upstairs in same design and color. She invested heavily in authentic paintings as an investment and finding two of Koa's paintings pleased her. She hoped he would see them one day hanging on her walls. She chose newest stereo system with tape deck, turn table with speakers neatly hidden in the wall. She also chose elaborate television console. She then longed for someone to share her fun but she pushed herself to continue on alone in her shopping. For her porches she chose white wicker and rattan with blue floral cushions downstairs and black and white stripes for porch furniture upstairs. Gray deck paint protected her floors. She especially selected a long table and chairs to seat Claire and her family for anticipated gatherings. She nearly blew Malcolm and Monique's minds when her brass king-size bed with oval headboard arrived, but she created hilarious laughter when she chose black linens with white abstract print with black bedspread and white and black dust ruffle and black with white pillow shams with several throw pillows of black, some white, some blue and some beige. Her triple black dresser with large mirror suited the decor and her matching chest of drawers gave her space to keep her mementos out of sight. The small bedroom was copy of hers but double brass bed, without blue chaise lounge, just a nice rocker. Her window treatment included ivory blinds and same white sheers as downstairs. The two nightstands of ebony set off her white lamps of milk bone china. Her reading area was the lounge and brass pole lamp. Her business would be conducted at dining table if necessary.

After her cabin was completed and filled with furniture, Sophee set out to choose cookware, flatware, china, crystal, silverware and towels, blue for downstairs and black and white for upstairs. She was creating a shrine to spinsterhood at its best. She made many trips to buy things she had forgotten. She had not concerned herself with cleaning and she laughed at her oversight without having to explain what caused the forgetfulness. Buying groceries was scheduled event after she moved from the cottage. She had received acknowledgments from her first dinner guests and that they would arrive at eight on the night she had chosen and all would be in formal attire. She selected her special music, planned her menu and shopped for special formal to dazzle her guests.

As she looked at her reflection in the mirror at "Ken's Formals", she knew she would never achieve desired look of sophistication with her blonde baby curls and tight ringlets but she promised to try. The sales lady showed her how to pin it up and leave ringlets along each side of her face. She smiled at the effort, but it helped a little. She settled on blue satin strapless and a diamond necklace and matching earrings for show, which added glamour and concealed the lack of sophistication. She felt she could afford to spoil herself since she felt she deserved a token of appreciation for deciding to carry the heavy load of the Tillers legacy and heritage alone. Her matching blue silk heels showed off her height at five feet ten inches. Succumbing to high powered showmanship, she bought expensive perfume and an evening purse for future use.

Sophee had worked secretly and had not announced her plans about the cabin. She let folks find out through small town communication. She had kept it a secret when she visited Claire who never asked her about it. She knew Jeremiah, Jason nor Latrelle would give away her secret until she publicly announced her plans. They kept secrets through pride and love, not money. They thrived on protecting her to carry on what Uncle Abram had inherited from his brother. No one at work knew, but questions would be asked when she asked for week off to landscape when weather was right for planting and to add her access road instead of driving around the pasture and to bring out yard furniture after planting.

Ambitious Hans had dumped Sophee and her heritage in his brother's lap. She missed Uncle Abram but Jeremiah was as efficient as his father but she missed the special love Uncle Abram always showered on her above all others. The group would force Drum to keep Sophee's affairs in the office. She had no reason to be secretive but she preferred to create entirely on her own and she pampered her selfish attitudes.

Her choice steaks, delicious thick prime rib-eyes, were marinating in the refrigerator. The baking potatoes wrapped in foil were almost ready for consumption. The steamed asparagus tips were in the pot and the cheese sauce in its own private dish was beside it. The tossed salad was being chilled and the salad dressing was in its serving carafe. The rolls from the bakery were on baking sheet ready to be popped into the oven after steaks were broiled. The apple pie, also from the bakery, was sliced and ready to be served a la mode with vanilla ice cream. Sour cream and butter were in special containers in the refrigerator. Steak sauces and salt and pepper shakers would be placed on the table after guests arrived.

Her blue napkins embossed with "Sophee" in white were waiting near white bone china to set table. Ice was in its chest with tongs near. The tea was in its pitcher. The coffee was already perked and ready, awaiting creamer and sugar. Sophee agonized over every item and felt foolish with her minute planning of each silly course of her first dinner at home. She hoped never to endure such trauma but as therapy dictated that she change, so indeed she would, at her expense.

Everything promised to be perfect when her first guest was Emily Jackson, dressed in long navy lace dress with jacket. It was a tearful scene even though they kept in touch. She placed her housewarming gift on the kitchen counter. Before Sophee could enjoy being alone with Emily, Brent in black suit and bow tie and Netta Jelks in black satin, arrived and Netta, her mama also, and Sophee shared same tearful reunion, although as with Emily, they stayed in touch. Brent placed their housewarming gift on the counter beside Emily's. Sophee loved the way her cabin looked. She had turned on all the lights to convince guests she was at home waiting for them. Malcolm arrived in black suit and bow tie with large plant in brass container. She hugged him and surprisingly he kissed her on her cheek, and placed the gift on the floor. Sophee greeted Monique, gowned in black silk, and while she was hugging her, she saw Koa, resplendent in white coat and black pants and tie, standing in her door with a very large present in his hands. His penetrating grey eyes were soft as she hugged him in the same loving manner she had hugged the others, and she almost forgot to breathe as he hugged her. She rejoiced that he was taller than she even in her heels. He leaned his present against the cabinet and Sophee made the proper introductions. She led her guests on the tour of new cabin, to her a mansion. Making themselves at home, Malcolm began the steaks and kissed Sophee again when he saw the seventh one for some uninvited guest and the extra potato. Within minutes dinner was on the table with flat silver bowl with blue carnations as her centerpiece. The flowers were a special contribution from the florist. Sophee turned off bright lights and turned on soft reflected ones. She turned on her music and was satisfied everything she had planned had turned out perfect.

While the ladies and Koa talked over coffee, Malcolm and Brent cleared the table and stacked dishes in the new dish washer. She was anxious to open her presents although she had been surprised at getting them, even if it was her first housewarming.

Sophee smiled at Malcolm and Monique as he picked up her plant and headed for her bedroom. Brent asked, "How did you know she wanted that in her bedroom? You two have a secret we should share?"

Malcolm laughed and sheepishly explained, "It was the only thing I could think of to match that gosh-awful big brass bed of hers."

Sophee laughed as he rushed back down the steps. Sophee embraced Emily as she began to open her gift. It was her scrap book Emily had faithfully and laboriously kept for her to at least represent her background enabling her to plant her roots. Sophee grinned at all the blimpey pictures of her obese frame, her long straight hair and Aunt Gerta's uniforms in her school picture. There were many happy scenes of her and uncle Abram which choked her. There were hers and Rick's wedding pictures and her pictures of the thin Sophee in uniform of her country which Sophee had sent to Emily. Sophee held back the tears as she hugged her and held on until she could function. She was not ready to face the past, but Emily didn't know. It was Sophee's to keep since it was her life. Love would overcome hurt. The two had come through hell together and still in functioning bodies and capable minds. The others watched and remained calm.

Netta and Brent had given her an eleven by twenty picture in a beautiful brass antiqued frame of the two of them. She embraced both of them and almost cried, but she did manage to thank them profusely. She had deliberately saved Koa's present until last, but when she found his to be his cherished house plans, autographed and framed under glass, tears formed but were wiped away as she hugged him again. She was almost speechless as she said, "This drawing is mine without any strings?"

Koa smiled, "As long as it hangs on your wall with other two paintings you have so wisely purchased."

His double meaning no longer angered her so she smiled and ushered her guests into her living room where animated conversations began among the people who were involved somehow in Sophee's life—past, present, and future. During the evening, Sophee demanded the floor, "The purpose in inviting you here tonight to my first housewarming is to Emily, who has always served as my mama and best friend and ally. To Netta, to whom I owe my life since through a small miracle she succeeded where everything else failed, she did it not for glory nor money which she refused but she felt it her christian duty for which I am truly thankful. To Brent, the understanding husband who helped care for their own children while Netta, his wife, attended me. A person could not ask for more. To Malcolm, who has remained a true friend who stands in as brother. In spite of all the heavy demands I heap on him because of my inexperience and ignorance of building and living, he has never lost his temper, to me, that is. To his charming wife, Monique, the best cook in the county, who offers shoulder on which to lean and to cry on and most of all she makes Malcolm happy. She is also going to give him a child."

They applauded and congratulated Malcolm who blushed and only smiled.

Sophee continued, "I guess, Koa, you are here since I ran out at your first evaluation of me. In accepting your drawing, I accept you but not your ultimatum. Thank you for returning."

She let the tears run freely down her face as she extended her hands toward them, enveloping them in her embrace, "Thank you for honoring me with your presence and your gifts. The door is always open to you. I even hear the fish are biting in the stream."

Her speech had interrupted them temporarily but the voices soon could be heard. They left too soon but as Koa stood in line to be last to leave, he gave her a small note and left with the others. She turned off all the lights except one in the kitchen and began another pot of coffee. She opened the note and read, "I'll be here at six to prepare breakfast and talk. Koa." She dropped the note in her cookie jar and smiled, turned out the light and went up for bed.

She felt lost in her large bed but she slept soundly even after the extra coffee which delayed her sleep. She awoke at five and felt excited. She would learn all about her stranger. She was pulling on her sweat shirt to match her jeans after showering when her doorbell rang. She wrapped the towel around her head and rushed downstairs to answer it. She looked through her peephole and seeing Koa standing there, she opened the door. They looked at each other and Koa stepped across the threshhod and entered her kitchen and Sophee felt at home.

Koa placed his hands rigidly against his thighs, "Before we can become friends, I must tell you how sorry I am if I frightened you with my arrogance at our first meeting. I misjudged you. Forgive me?"

Sophee looked steadily at him and smiled, "Won't you come in? Yes, Koa, I forgive you. I acted childish by running. Forgive me."

"We are now friends since both are forgiven for acting like a couple of kids on their first date." He looked around as if looking for something he missed the night before.

Sophee asked, "Why are you here so early? It is only five thirty."

Koa looked at her towel-wrapped head and said calmly, "I thought you would get up early, which you did, and do something foolish like cooking since I wanted to cook for us. It has been a while since I cooked in a kitchen with enough space to move about."

Koa sensed she had confused feeling about their first meeting which affected her perhaps as it had affected him. Sophee motioned toward the kitchen as she said, "Make the coffee first before you begin cooking. Ask for anything you can't find and I'll have to tell you I haven't bought that item yet. Last night was my first night here and I don't know what I bought and what I brought from the cottage. I wasn't frightened by you, just the inference of marriage scared me and I did what I do best, I ran."

Koa said while preparing coffee, "I have had my share of running, either to or from something or me but I feel it is too soon for you to trust me about those days. Let's have breakfast first and then after the morning sun warms up everything, we will take an inspection of the clearing and talk if we want to talk or just walk and enjoy the view."

Sophee spoke rather fast, "I don't usually talk but I will listen, since my imagination of your exciting life in the van is quite bazaar. I must finish drying my hair." While he watched her rub the towel to dry her hair, she finished and tossed the towel in the laundry and closed the door.

Koa leaned toward her and raised his hand as if to touch her hair. He paused, "May I?"

She nodded and leaned her had so she could not see his eyes as he gently touched her damp curls and being amazed at its softness, he ran his fingers through her hair, patted it and said, "It is so soft. Is it natural?"

She laughed, "I do not think this style can be duplicated. With any kind of cut, it looks the same. I certainly wouldn't pay for having it look like this."

"It suits you. I like its color and its curl."

"You have been outdoors too long! But thank you."

He turned and poured their coffee. She took her cup and led him to her front porch. She looked at her surroundings and felt her cabin was an excellent decision even if it endangered any future with Koa whose stability was as fragile as hers. They sat in the love seat and set their coffee cups on the table. He was not demonstrating any intentions. Each sat and remained silent, taking in the beauty around them. Finally Koa chuckled, "I guess you built this cabin so you could live here alone without considering marriage?"

She looked at him, took a sip of coffee, replaced her cup on the table and answered, "Not really Koa. It is not that simple. I built it in desperation. I have a debilitating fear of being rejected and when I suffer being pushed into a rut or groove or if I allow myself dare to let my hair down and let my feelings show and allow emotion to exert some control and dare to trust people or simply to endure an internal combustion of not being wanted, necessary or needed, whether intended or by accident, I pack and leave with no remorse for those I leave behind. I go without a conscience. I can't consider marriage under those circumstances. I hope my cabin and my land become a permanent yoke. I need to land."

He looked at the water in the stream and then looked at her, "Do you have any hobbies?"

Sophee looked at him thoughtfully, "Not really. I only hope to learn to enjoy feeling. I only learned to dance recently, which I enjoyed. Nothing dictates to me and I don't appreciate unfinished business, like a knitted sweater that was never sleeved, a poem of only three lines or a semi-blank canvas. I lack personal discipline since I am always running like a fugitive. If I don't begin something, I don't have to worry about the finished product that would enforce a premature return."

Koa looked at the water which was so peacefully still as he said, "I drive my van and paint and that's all I have. When my wife, my parents, our two daughters and only son and my faithful dog perished in a house fire, I settled my affairs, bought my van and hit the roads and by ways. By selling everything, I hoped I would not find a reason to return, so I don't look back over my shoulder to see if I left anything. I have been running for ten years and see so chance of changing. I even changed my profession. My hobby is how I earn my living. I can't get close to anyone. I sometimes communicate my disturbed feelings onto a canvas and erase most of it when I return to a normal state and recognize the madness on the canvas. Ladies have loved me but I couldn't return their love. I have been searching for normal state of living and for the soul that was lost. I have been running so long that I haven't visited their graves. I blamed me for not dying with them. They took everything that was worthwhile with them. I probably would not recognize what I was looking for. I could stumble over it and keep on looking. We are a pair."

Sophee touched his arm, "My friend, Claire, constantly tells me, 'Wherever you may decide to roam, Sophee, when you get halfway there, return to your roots, here on the land, since what you are leaving is what you are seeking, yourself and your heritage.' It somehow does not work for me. I am still running and it hurts to know you are different from the masses."

Koa stood, "It is such a beautiful day, let's leave it undisturbed. I am hungry."

Sophee stood, "You are the cook, but I'll help since I contributed to the delay. I am hungry too. I suppose that is one sign that we perhaps are a wee bit normal."

Koa laughed as he commented, "Every little thing will show us the way back."

CHAPTER THIRTEEN

Koa did not look out of place in Sophee's kitchen. She drank coffee while he mixed batter for pancakes and kept the sausage patties turned so they would not burn. He left the centerpiece where it was and set the juice glasses and plates already served on the table and refilled their coffee cups.

Sophee was surprised that the pancakes were delicious. They discussed the weather, economy, politics and the stately oaks and many simple things but hedged on bringing personal lives to the breakfast table before they finished eating.

Sophee asked, "Who taught you how to cook? You are better than I am at pancakes."

"I learned on my own when I began my gypsy life. I was a selfish husband. I let my wife do all the work in the home. I felt when I married her, housework was her responsibility like it had been my mother's and my grandmothers. We married while still in college and both of us worked. She was filled with energy and could get her work done in short order. She was an illustrator of children's books and worked very hard. I was conceited enough to think that somehow I worked harder than she and it was her place to see to my needs and to care for the kids when they came. I don't see how she put up with me. It is too late for her but I am now aware of my past mistakes. We built a very large house and our parents visited often. I enjoyed reigning as king of the Declah household. I was manager of "Dewey's Tools and Supplies" that earned me a good salary and Nola brought home a large pay check. Both introduced us to many citizens in town. We had it all and we were happy and in love. Our home was where everyone loved to go and there were always parties with neighbors. Nola always cooked. The children copied our life style and filled the home with friends. Yet, there was church. We worked as hard for the Lord as we did for ourselves and our community, and I attended many art classes and sold several paintings and helped Nola with some of her illustrations. We were a team at some things."

Sophee looked down at her cup, "I have never lived in a happy family unit of my own. After the death of my parents, I lived with a very bitter and loveless Aunt and Uncle, my father's sister and her husband. I was cared for and nurtured by Emily who showered me with love, guidance and exposure to living. I loved Uncle Abram, daddy's brother. He loved me but had to show his love outside the home because of his mentally deranged sister. I nursed at Netta's breast since I could tolerate nothing else. I still love her. I did not establish a home with my two brief marriages. I lived alone in my parents' "Honeymoon Cottage", all without love and family. What you had was too precious to lose. I realize how awful it must have been for you. I admire the manner in which you are dealing with your sorrow. I hope you heal."

"I was attending a convention and my wife, sweet Nola, stayed home because she had two rush jobs to complete under deadline which happened often. Mom and Dad were leaving for home the day after the fire. The fire was believed by the officials to have started in the wiring in the attic. All of them died in their sleep from smoke inhalation. Before the flames burned them, the fire was brought under control. They didn't wake up. Evidently the dog died first before barking. He was old and stiff with arthritis but he was a true friend. It happened at three in the morning and no one in the neighborhood saw the smoke until it was too late. We lived just out of the city limits but had area fire department. It has been ten long years and I still miss them. The children would be teens and pre-teens by now with their personalities fully developed and Nola would be beautiful and successful. What a waste!"

Sophee placed her hand on top of Koa' s. Their eyes met as she said, "Perhaps I can make you let go with the past and lead you to a happy and fulfilling future. I am not suggesting we become an item. We deserve a second chance. Our suffering is similar in intensity."

"You would try? I don't accept strangers too easily."

"Yes I will try. I think it is worth a try if we decide it is for the best to restore our faith in ourselves. It is only the two of us. I have helped others readjust and renew their lives without getting involved. The last patient suggested I hang up my shingle and that I was in wrong profession."

"Thank you Sophee. I'll do my part but I know I will suffer for it."

Sophee smiled as she nodded and said, "And I'll do mine. I feel the timing is right. We will achieve happiness for both and hopefully stop each other from running. No strings are attached to proposal. You must be aware of that. I am not chasing you."

Koa spoke, "I am good at overlooking strings. I carry sharp scissors. Do you think we might be taking the easy and cowardly way by running? I have often thought there must be a better way. Have you ever considered making a stand by facing the problem and making it run instead of your running?"

Sophee said, "Koa, perhaps you already know everything about me because Malcolm loves to talk freely, but I was an inmate in three sanatoriums for the insane for three years. With all the counselling, and group therapy I have received, I can't force myself to confront my problem because it grows way out of proportion and overcomes my power of logical thinking. I can't push it aside. It overwhelms me. I only know to run to escape destruction. I am an alcoholic because of my inability to cope but I know from experience I can't drink, so I don't, but I still run without purpose and planned destination. I gave my child to a friend, Claire, who dried me out. She adopted him and eleven other children which strangely makes me happy and relieved. He is safe with her. He refers to me as mother and to Claire as mama, but he preferes the security of a home which I can't give him. He never associates with my cousins. My father chose suicide when my mother died shortly after my birth. About the only worthwhile things I can do without messing up is helping others and nursing children in pediatrics ward in any hospital. Both of my husbands divorced me. The first one was killed by a moving train that struck his stalled truck on the tracks. It was perhaps suicide. The second one did not think I had the proper bloodlines to carry on his name, yet his son wore his name until he was adopted. I must confess, I didn't love either. Both marriages were circumstantial. My best performance for a short while until I hit the bottle was as a nurse during the war. I shirk my responsibilities as owner of Tillers Estate because wealth frightens me."

Koa poured them the last of the coffee and while his back was turned to her, he asked, "Sophee, do you think you are incapable of love?"

Sophee trembled with fear of confessing that she had an awakening of unknown feelings the first time she saw him but she took a deep breath, exhaled and spoke, "I always thought I was until I saw you that night at Malcolm's. You arouse strange feeling that I have never felt before but I can't call it love."

He shrugged and said, "What would you call what you feel? Passion?"

Sophee laughed and didn't consider it might inflict pain. When she could stop laughing, she explained, "Definitely not passion. My first sexual encounter was reason for being committed to the psycho ward. My first sexual satisfaction resulted in marriage that lasted thirty minutes before being sued for divorce, but it produced my son. So what I am feeling is unknown to me. With time, I'll see what developes and I'll label it with its true identity and if not, I'll run."

Koa smiled at her, "What you are, is an honest woman who is just beginning to live, though scared silly. You excite me and yet aggravate me. When you do not take my advice, and your flagrant irresponsibility towards your heritage."

She looked into his piercing eyes which had not softened and asked, "You mean about the house? To build a cabin instead of negotiating with you for the house you designed? And allowing others to use my money?"

"Yes, that and that you deprive yourself of the many pleasures your money could provide. Spread your wings and reach for love. It just might make you content and happy enough to place yourself in the life of someone who returns that love."

She laughed, "It isn't Christmas but ho! ho! ho!"

He looked seriously at her, "How wealthy are you, Sophee? Do you really know?"

"Are you auditioning or just taking your place in line? I don't actually know and the more I spend the richer I get. I must be filthy rich since I am shunned by most people in town since I am not charitable but I give to my tenants which satifies me and them and I donate to the Church where I was recently baptized. I am not all bad but I am not all good either. Just the type to be taken as is or to be left alone."

He chuckled, "I think you are what I have been looking for but right now I want to spend time with you and become your friend. You arouse something in me but I am in no hurry to rush that emotion. I am only interested in resuming life as a man."

She studied his face, "You are saying that our relationship will be kept under glass like my house plans?"

He nodded, "Yes, that's exactly right."

She folded her arms, "What would you do if I removed the plans and used them?"

He never smiled as he answered, "Burn down your house and blame the ghosts who live there. You won't use them against my wishes, will you?"

She grinned, "No. I have my cabin, and Koa, only minutes ago you said I was an honest woman. I need your friendship more than the house. I have my cabin."

They looked at each other and each knew life was offering them a second chance but each knew it would take a long while to move freely, securely, and safely along the fragile come-back trail. Each had found the threat of the perfect yoke but old hurts detained them.

Koa explained, "I have some prior commitments that have to be met. Don't decide to run before I return. I won't call you but I'll bring choice steaks for our supper when I return."

She knew he was saying goodbye but she pretended he was making definite promises as she spoke, "I enjoyed having you here and if you plan to cook, bring all the fixings. I don't keep too much food here. I'll see you when you return. I'll be working at the hospital, visiting the county agent for farming hints and to get an idea of what to plant during planting season besides a garden and flowers, with Malcolm for teaching me how to farm and I will be here in the evenings after visiting Claire and her family. I try to see Hans every day."

Koa opened her back door and stood as if he really didn't want to leave her but he seemed driven by inner forces to depart quickly. He didn't kiss her goodbye. He said, "See you." and left.

Sophee spent the first week cleaning and painting the "Honeymoon Cabin." She left her parents' furnishings as they had left them. She washed all the linens and cleaned the drapes for new tenant. She washed and re-hung the curtains. The place was in excellent condition. She made both beds and as she closed the front door, her last look gave her a sad feeling of leaving home for the last time with no destination in mind.

She asked Jeremiah to rent out the cabin completely furnished to someone who would love living there as much as she had. It was time to say goodbye to the things that had kept her from having any one else live there. She realized her mistake in opening up to Koa in telling him too much which evidently frightened him. He was too disturbed to be a part of her future. She had learned a vital but painful lesson about love but not in vain, she would know how much to tell in the future, if she dared to consider love. A cycle had been broken and she could spread her wings as Koa had suggested.

She accepted dinner at Claire's for Saturday night and Church Sunday morning. She wanted to confide in Claire but the pain was too fresh to share. She shared friendship instead.

She pursued the normal events. She bought groceries and invited Malcolm and Monique over for supper. They had not heard from Koa. They promised to assist her in identifying the shrubbery and flowers growing near the clearing and to choose spots for well and septic tank and to repair damaged rock wall near the garden. She knew without Koa she would build permanent home. There were other architects who would please her. From the plat, Malcolm suggested best pasture land for beef cattle and he offered to string fence for the many separate pastures and upgrade existing pastures for her and build the necessary feeding areas, watering systems, barns, corrals and loading chutes. All three planned to attend auctions to buy her first cattle and to celebrate with dinner after unloading the animals since Malcolm would have their feed delivered and stored in the barns before the cattle arrived. She knew she depended too much on him but after she learned, she would help him and lighten his load.

The well they dug would furnish water to her designed house and to the barns and her garden restoration project. Since her horse "Zeus" was a social animal, she asked Malcolm to keep him with his horses. She wished to avoid creating loneliness for any animal since she knew its pain.

When the phone rang, Sophee became excited, hoping it was Koa since he had been gone nearly two months. It was Jeremiah who asked, "Do you have any reservations about Dr. Tharpe Gunter renting the cabin?"

She smiled thinking how much he had changed. She said, "That would be perfect. Could you very diplomatically include as many acres of land for him to have something to keep him busy without adding more to the rent?"

He cleared his throat and asked, "Were you two ever involved?"

"Would it matter? But no. He was about ready to snap when he returned to town. I pulled him back in line. We aren't even friends now. He finds it difficult to accept my status. He is a new man through my generous counselling. I am glad Tharpe wants to live there. He will be near Claire, Schwinn, who have become his friends, and the children."

Jeremiah paused for a while and asked, "If you aren't interested in Tharpe, won't you please mingle and look for a mate here in Longbranch? I am sure you can find an eligible bachelor who would prove suitable as a companion. You have been alone long enough and you need to produce legal heirs to inherit the Estate. It is up to you and you alone to guarantee the continued legacy. Hans needs siblings to share the awesome responsibility."

She listened but could not give him his answers or solutions, "I know, but I am happy as I am. I agree with you. Tillers Estate needs heirs as well as my cooperation in its operation. Come to dinner after Church Sunday. Bring Latrelle, Jason and Sarah. You can see my efforts developing as a farmer under Malcolm's supervision, of course. I am learning and you will appreciate that I am keeping an accurate set of books. Be prepared to tell me of the little things I can ease into in lifting Jason's awesome tasks of taking over Tillers Estate as you did from Uncle Abram. I don't know why I am assuming such hard work but I am ready. I know it is way over due. See you right after Church. Call Tharpe and tell him I am happy knowing he will be in the cabin. Jeremiah, you need a little relaxation, be prepared to fish. I have a boat you can take out to find your own solitude."

"Your heart is showing. We'll see you Sunday."

CHAPTER FOURTEEN

Tillers Memorial Medical Center was operating with good profits. Residents from nearby towns had been choosing to use their staff and facilities. It was always filled to capacity. There had been no snags. Schwinn used her visits to the sheep farm to hold their meetings as before. He was experienced and very capable and Sophee gave him authority to act for her which eliminated delays. She stayed informed.

The hospital was getting publicity since doctors had requested to observe some of their techniques. Sophee stood in awe at having world re-known doctors on her staff who accepted their colleagues' invitation to observe. She took no credit for its success beyond getting it in Longbranch since it had been so necessary to bring care to the citizens of the area.

Sophee had built several apartment complexes for the many employees and professional buildings for offices for the staff to live near their work and bring in consultants. She ventured after she found hospital could operate successfully. She added another dorm for the nurses and technicians near the hospital. She brought in a florist and a pharmacy to accommodate patients. Provisions were made for relatives of very ill patients to live in special apartment complex during critical care. Her town was not very large but she wanted care to exceed any hospital. She was a bit egotistical and erected a Tillers sign on all buildings.

Sophee ran into her first brick wall. Malcolm was adamant in his refusal to work with turkeys when she informed him of planning a turkey hatchery and farm for marketing adult turkeys throughout the year since climate was conducive to their growth and capability of enduring proper growth on her farm. She felt like crying, but she asked, "What is wrong with turkeys?"

He raised his voice and threw up his hands, "They are stupid and too noisy and they take too much time and space in keeping them healthy and fat. What do you know about them? Can you operate an incubator in your hatchery?"

She shouted, "Woa! Woa there! Just one minute! They are smart birds. They gobble loudly when disturbed. With proper equipment and management, no more time is needed for them than for chickens. We are a good team and are smart enough to raise anything. Even a little hell. Everyone has chickens. Get me a man or woman or a family to live here and take care of both operations. I'll offer them a good deal. I will build a house for them and we can tie in to my well and septic tank. We can have everything ready for operation within a few weeks with you and the Tillers' crew on the job. Unless you want the job?"

He laughed, "No thanks. My feelings haven't changed. You need to find Koa and push him around instead of me. I'll get the workers. I will see that your houses and barns and covered runways are built for your "smart" birds. You order your hatching equipment and request an expert to set up its operation. Tell me what you need and I will get a turkey farmer for you. It might take longer than you anticipate, but I'll begin immediately. You need to concern yourself with a nursery like me and Monique. Someone needs to calm you down."

She smiled, "Thank you for going against your feeling to help me get my "smart" bird farm a reality. I have considered having a baby, Malcolm, and bringing it up alone. How do you think the citizens of Longbranch would react if I decided to have three babies by artificial insemination, without being married and not knowing who the fathers might be. Your answer is expected at end of our turkey conversation."

"Thank you, let's stick with turkeys."

She smiled at his shocked expression, "Please help me decide what kind of cow feed and turkey feed I can grow and what knid of vegetables and flowers I can grow here on my little stretch. Please don't get angry. I need you and Monique to continue as my friends. Don't let birds come between us! I am lonesome as hell. You two are all I have."

He touched her shoulder, "Don't worry. You will have us and your birds but I will have to think about your having your babies without a husband. I could whip Koa for skipping out. Sorry, little one, if you were upset over how I feel about raising turkeys but I can find ways to work around my dislike. They aren't the only things I dislike about farming. I would rather have birds than some critters, I have never seen the kind of operation you want but we'll set it up and enjoy maximum production, together, as always."

She smiled, "Thank you friend. Be as expedient and efficient as usual and I'll be happy. You get a turkey for every Thanksgiving dinner and Christmas, and when a child is born or whenever Monique wants to have turkey on her table." She looked at her watch, "Late again. Good day, we will talk about the babies later. I must run. I am meeting with Jeremiah, Drum and Jason to take over some of the operation of Tillers and move into office I rented beside Jeremiah's office. They can wait. I can't wait any longer for your answer to my suggestion about having three babies."

Malcolm raked his hand down his face, looked at Sophee, took off his hat, ran his fingers through his beautiful black, thick hair, replaced his hat on his head and pushed the dirt around with the toe of his boot and looked at her and smiled as he began his answer. "They won't like you any more or any less. You belong to us at Tillers and we would support your decision and love you a little bit more."

Sophee wiped away a tear and said, "Thank you. I hoped I'd keep your love."

Malcolm asked, "You have already decided, haven't you? When and where will you get it done?"

"In Stratford Clinic when I decide time is right. I must qualify legally, but I can't wait much longer if I get the three I want. I will tell you and Monique all about it when I set it up. It will cost a bundle but I am sure my dear old daddy would approve."

He asked, "You really don't want marriage, do you?"

"No. I am not cut out for marriage but I feel I have matured sufficiently to have children. The estate needs heirs. I'll have to build a house with more bedrooms or add on rooms to the cabin. I like where my cabin is located and the comfort it gives me, so I might choose to build in the clearing and live with the ghosts."

He smiled, "That's logical thinking. I hope it works."

She smiled, "It's guaranteed."

"I am happy for you."

"Thanks. Maybe I should have a duck operation, then we would all waddle."

"Get to your meeting!"

Claire, in understanding how Sophee's mind worked, waited until she was invited to visit her cabin and observe her farm techniques. Claire calmly accepted her invitation over the phone and waited to jump for joy after hanging up the phone.

The hamburgers and hot dogs were already cooked, the onions diced, chili was heated, cole slaw, pickles relish and sauerkrout were ready in refrigerator. Ketchup, mustard, and mayonnaise were ready to place on the table. Buns were on baking sheets, ready to heat. A large container of french fries was being kept warm. The table on the front porch downstairs was set for sixteen places and two platters of fruit tarts were in the center of the table. Several gallons of lemonade were being chilled.

On the counter was a basket of letters for sticking on clothing. As Sophee greeted them, she asked that each one fasten a letter where it could be seen with ease. She was thrilled in showing Claire her cabin. The children were working to make a message out of the letters. Martha and Ernest, the twins, solved the puzzle and had all children to stand in order of message, "Welcome to my Home." Sophee gave Martha a pack of bird cards and Ernest a picture book of animals. Sophee loved the noise the children made.

Schwinn escaped by taking the children outdoors while Sophee and Claire cleared the table and swept up the crumbs after the exciting supper. When the two returned to the kitchen for coffee, Claire asked, "Why have you done all this?"

Sophee looked into her dear friend's eyes, "To keep me here where everyone says I belong. I give my notice next week to the hospital so someone who needs the money and can work. I am taking on full operation at Tillers after I learn how it works. Malcolm doesn't know it yet but he is to become an officer to assist me and he must also become my manager. I must bribe him with a farm he has been longing for. He can do both jobs. He needs to own his own land now that their first baby is coming. He is like a brother to me. He earned his degree in agriculture and has never let anyone know. I knew he left the farm to go to college. Monique told me after I told her of my plans for him. He will pay me back since he is very proud and pays for what he gets. Nothing is free to him."

Claire observed Sophee, "What is really bothering you Sophee? I can tell you still want to hit new ground but you are forcing yourself to stay here against your will to run and not stay put. What is it or who is it?"

Sophee sipped her coffee and smiled, "I think I am in love with a stranger who is afraid to feel and loves to run more than I ever did. His suffering is very obvious. He is a successful artist. He painted those two pictures in the living room and designed the house that hangs as a picture on the wall—under glass like him. To give him a chance to make right decision about us, I told him just about everything. Something in my report must have scared him off permanently. He has been gone three months without any contact. Nothing was between us but a feeling of something that could be there if nurtured."

Claire looked around the cozy kitchen, "So you are saddling yourself with too much work so you will be forced to stay on the land."

"Yes. There are days when I love what I am doing but when the urge takes over, I suffer and dread the outcome. I don't think Koa is coming back to me. I need someone all my own. I work harder and get through an hour at a time. I have become too involved with the land to walk away ever again. In assuming command, I feel free to expand. Malcolm hates turkeys but he is setting up equipment and houses for the turkey farm I am planning to operate at a booming profit. He has the designs for the houses for the incubator area and for the houses for the varying sizes of growing and adult birds to be marketed. We pour over brochures and make many phone calls to egg farms to markets and the local grocery stores and carriers to move birds in large quantities. Everything is falling in its proper place except Koa. Claire, what I have really decided which frightens me but consoles me is to have three children by artificial insemination since I don't look to find a man to love me. I am ready for motherhood now. I'll have to work, as you know, but I can find a nanny here on Tillers land. Do you think I can be a good mother after failing so miserably with Hans?"

"Yes, Sophee. You are now mature enough to handle it. It isn't easy. Motherhood will be more confining than your birds. You still need something to hold you here, don't you?"

Claire asked, "Does Koa know about Rick, Drake and Hans?"

"Yes. I told him about all the decent things I did, not my deeds of my gutter days. He need not know everything even if we marry. We can live with what he knows. I might have scared him too much for him to return. His parents, wife and children were killed in a home fire about ten years ago, and his dog. He still talks about how beautiful his wife Nola would be today if she had lived."

"You may love him and he may love you, but together each might lean too much on the other. That doesn't sound promising for happiness which you both deserve. What would happen if both of you decided to run at same time? As long as you are involved with your heritage at last, happiness will sneak up on you and you will not know when desire to run has been cured and you will not need Koa or any man as a crutch. Have faith. If it is meant to be, he will return to you. Don' t give up on him, but have your children. You always came back. Don't even consider what folks hereabouts might say about you, just do it for you and the children."

"Yes, you are right, and I kept leaving until now. Thank you for your good ear. I will keep you informed about my planned babies. Now, lets visit Eden, the spot that keeps me here. The children can fish after we walk over and see the beef herds. I laugh as I look at my white cattle, my black cattle and my red cattle. If I could find blue cattle, I would name the farm "Independence.""

Claire laughed, "At least you see humor in farming."

"Without Malcolm, I am still me, not too good at anything. I plan to change all that. I work late at night, studying about farming, turkey raising and large investments and stocks. Fatigue helps me sleep. I shock easily. The incubators can hatch one hundred thousand baby turkeys every twenty-eight days. That boggles my mind."

"I have faith in you even if you are overdoing it. Thankfully you can stagger the operation and keep in control. I always dread lambing time since so many are born at once, I cry when a lamb dies. You will probably cry over your dead turkeys. It seems such a waste. I want to save them all. We can't win over nature."

"I know but in knowing, it doesn't stop us from trying."

Claire smiled, "Dr. Gunter says you are in wrong profession. You should open up your guidance clinic since he feels you are responsible for his total recovery. Apply your knowledge to yourself, something of which you practice on others. Now that you have kept me at a safe distance long enough, can we make this our second home? Schwinn would enjoy helping with the incubators when you begin your hatchery. He hails from the turkey state of the nation. Ask him, okay? You need some sound of live human voices here."

"Yes, I do. Silence sometimes chokes me. Claire, Schwinn is doing an outstanding job at the hospital. He is in charge and everyone knows it. Without him, there would be no organized method of doing anything. Let him know I think he is super efficient and the center's success is his. I need him. If he wants a hand in hatching turkey eggs, I will see that he has plenty to do. I am glad you two got back together."

"Me too. Sophee, I am complete for the first time in my life and I am not working outside the home which I always thought would be the last thing I gave up. I still bless the day we met."

Sophee smiled, "Let's don't get teary-eyed, you can't see my three colors of cattle that Malcolm purchased. I'll have Malcolm and Monique over on your next visit. You will love them as I do."

When Claire reached the clearing, she was speechless. Schwinn joined them. "Everything that makes a home is here except the house. Have you researched the history of this land?"

"No but I fell in love with it at first sight."

He laughed as he danced a few steps of a waltz, "The orchestra can begin the music any minute as we stroll through the ball room admiring the lovely ladies and gallant gentlemen. I love it."

Sophee shared his nostalgia as she began explaining, "I have been working in the garden here. We have identified the plants and flowers. We are pruning, weeding and planting to bring back their original beauty and design. When we see something that blends, we add that since there are many spaces that needed replanting. We are working on the rock wall. That's something you and the children can do. Haul the rocks that are found among the plants back to the wall and help restore it. There is so much to do to bring it back to its original beauty. Malcolm begs me not to work alone because of the large snakes, so it is not every day we can get out here. Monique is good with plants and she is teaching me to restore the beds. We want to do it ourselves instead of having it done professionally which would destroy our human touch. The trees are very old and one day I'll find out how old they really are but for now I don't have a spare minute."

Schwinn looked around, he asked, "You are planning to build on this site, aren't you?"

Sophee smiled at Schwinn's excitement, "Yes. Just as soon as designer of my house returns."

"Could I have some input into its design? That would please me greatly."

"You bet, but it will be a while. I am restoring the garden that won't be in the path of builders. By the time the designer returns, I'll have my new farm in complete operation so you might be able to have lots of input in the designing. Malcolm will need an extra pair of hands now and especially when the incubator arrives. When you get a minute, just hop on over. The idea of so many baby turkeys to be placed in their houses frightens me but I'll do it with help. Poor Malcolm, he actually hates turkeys, but for me he is helping me get it going. His college pal with his wife and four kids will be arriving in thirty days. They are discussing house plans so when we get the green light, workers from Tillers Estate who need extra money will probably have the house ready for occupancy by the time they arrive. Come over for that, too, if you like."

Schwinn spoke, "You sound excited—like this is what you want."

Sophee smiled at him, "I had never considered what being a Tillers involved. I guess one could say I have been a spoiled brat and very childishly selfish. They gave up everything and came to this country. Dad loved this section of America and he tried to buy the whole county, not knowing he would leave it to someone like me who has never cared a tinker's dam about land before but now I am in the process of making amends and so far it has proved to be a welcome yoke."

Schwinn asked her, "Does this mean you will be a full time farmer and give up your nursing job at the hospital?"

Sophee nodded and waited for his reaction, "Not a full time, full-time farmer. I am taking over entire operation of Tillers and also farm. I plan to give my notice of resignation Monday, as I just told Claire and she approves."

Schwinn smiled, "As Claire has always said, your roots are here and you didn't know it, but I am happy for you. We'll miss you at the hospital. Once you become dedicated to something, you really go one hundred percent, even in leaving. Good luck and I'll miss seeing you. I'll come here for our meetings on the way home and will probably find my family here also."

Sophee held his arm, "Schwinn, please feel free to take part in any phase of my new business here. Believe me, you are needed. I only wish you were a veterinarian."

CHAPTER FIFTEEN

After six months had passed and no sign of Koa, Sophee decided he wasn't returning. She thought of him every time she looked at the framed house plans. Doug and Wally Mehon with their children, Sosebee, Sybil, Zack and Yevette had moved into their new house and they were awaiting the first batch of turkeys to hatch. It had been an exciting experience in choosing the eggs since Sophee decided to raise the first batch to see percentage of survival and sell baby turkeys as well as the mature birds. To maintain her color scheme on the farm, she had chosen the bronze turkey, the kind that grew up to fifty pounds for males and up to sixteen pounds for females. She chose the Small White for consumption all year because of its size. It was white and the males grew up to twenty-three pounds and females a popular eleven pounds. She chose the black turkey because of its color. The males grew up to thirty-three pounds and the females up to fourteen pounds. She had chosen to house her birds to protect them from chilling rains and predators with her initiation. Everything else was automatic. The houses were ready with feeders and watering devices and cooling and heating since it was tedious going at first since they grew so fast. She gave them music to relax which gave Malcolm something more to laugh at her about.

Doug had worked at hatchery before so Sophee relaxed and let her tension come unwound. Schwinn spent many hours with Doug and replaced straw from the houses like a pro. Doug hired laborers from families on Tillers' Estate to keep houses clean and hopefully free of diseases. The vet, Dr. Trotson, was very cooperative and dropped by to bring Sophee new literature. The county agent had shown interest in her new industry, the first in the county. Dale McNeeley was impressed with Sophee's knowledge of turkey farming and cattle raising. He liked the variety of vegetables and spices in her garden. He need not know she mouthed many empty words and found out their meaning after he left. Emily spent many nights with Sophee and enjoyed sleeping on the small brass bed. She even felt she owed Sophee something for her house that she had bought for her. Netta dropped in with her grand children and she also felt indebted to Sophee for her home, but Sophee tried to convince them that life itself as Emily and Netta had sustained was a small exchange.

Sophee felt elated when she took her home-grown corn, wheat, soybeans and sorghum to be ground for feed and gloated with her new knowledge as she requested protein supplements, vitamins and meat by products to be added. The more she moved about the community, the more she was noticed. It was difficult to tell she was a woman. The vet gave her drugs to add to her birds' feed and water and as long as no disease occurred, he would not vaccinate them. She informed him that as a nurse she could assist him. She sold most of the birds from all her houses and then bought eggs for second hatching. She mixed the birds in the open pens and thoroughly cleaned the houses for her second babies. Doug kept accurate records. His only liability was in preferring not to talk. He worked quietly and that's all he wanted.

Martin Petrie chose to make his entrance into the world on a cold and rainy night, only minutes after Malcolm, Doug and Sophee had taken the new birds to the barn and had watched over them to determine their start at their rapid growth. Sophee and Doug worked while Malcolm drove Monique to Tillers Medical Center. Wally sat by the phone to get the message after the baby arrived and both were fine. After a night without sleep, Doug and Sophee were brought the news at daylight that Martin had arrived and he and his father were fine as reported by the mother.

Hoping to assure Emily that she was needed, Sophee left her at the cabin to answer the phone and take orders for her birds and to assist in any emergency while she met with Dr. Traveckie at the clinic for the great moment. After legalizing her intentions, she had been examined and tested for all probabilities of anything going wrong to prevent the birth of a healthy baby. In matching her physical make up, the energetic staff had suggested male composites so child would look familiar to her. Her stay in the clinic had been short and the procedure well organized and very dignified. She felt the same but very anxious. She waited for positive results.

The moment she knew she was pregnant, she gave thanks. Dr. Traveckie assured her she would have a happy pregnancy and a healthy baby if she followed his instructions. He also convinced her the extra weight gain would slow her down but it would be temporary.

She had enjoyed travelling to the homes of various farmers to sell them on turkey raising. She advertised and sold nearly all the turkey babies, her pet name, before they were hatched. Within weeks she had succeeded in selling all her poults. She secured names and sold by phone, using magazines, newspapers and radio for contacts. She levelled off at point of production that could be handled easily with her and her crew.

Her feeders were ready for market so she wanted to be in the middle of the hustle and excitement. Everything was growing. She learned vegetables, when ripe, waited for no one. She hired laborers to gather, clean, and prepare the vegetables for canning, cooking, and home freezing, a new craze. She sweated and laughed. She was always dirty and worked long hours but never found it embarrassing.

Her best advertising was coming from satisfied customers. When word spread through the county where a healthy bird could be bought, many people came directly to the farm and sent their friends. Her new venture was rapidly developing into type of organization she had wanted. She finally wore a feathered yoke and hopefully permanent. When she cemented lucrative contracts, on her own initiative, for thousands to be shipped, she was almost delirious but too pregnant to jump for joy. She spent lots of money to develop well organized operation but if she succeeded, money would have provided excellent investment. She was learning how money worked and was appreciating how to make more for herself and Tillers Estate.

Claire was shipping her sheep through same truck lines and the drivers gave a good tally of what their businesses were doing. Sophee yearned to grant her residents on Tillers' land recognition in Longbranch that they were people who belonged. She printed flyers she had prepared about next notice of farm meeting in town. She stuffed them in all their mailboxes and called on them, urging them to attend and be recognized in the community for what they were. They owned their land on which their homes were built and farmed many acres of land. She wanted to inform the townspeople that they were concerned about the future of farming in Longbranch.

She attended with Malcolm and Monique and Martin, and her dear friends, Claire and Schwinn and her newcomers, Doug and Wally. She was shocked and proud to hear Malcolm address the crowd. They listened to his ideas and she approved of his calm, relaxed and intellectual manner and approach. There was no important issue on the agenda but she hoped many would return. Gunter's parents greeted her. She hoped they would visit families outside the comfort and security of Tillers and exchange ideas and broaden their interests. The men were hesitant in accepting women but she could improve that. She and Claire had dared to bring new industry to Longbranch and succeeding at their endeavors was a bit unsettling to the men who hesitated to try new ideas. Sophee decided to give them a second chance to accept women as their equals. During refreshments, the men invited Sophee, Monique, Wally and Claire to come to the next meeting. They laughed about crashing the place but planned to attend all of the meetings to let them know there were female farmers in the county who made money.

CHAPTER SIXTEEN

Just prior to showing with her first baby, Sophee, Monique and her baby, Martin, in his carriage, were working in the garden. They were dirty and happy since both had grown to love the beauty of their work and it was something Monique could enjoy with Martin. She was very possessive and kept him with her always. Over their chatter, they heard a car engine just briefly. They thought it was a customer so they left the matter with Doug and Wally who were with the birds. Malcolm was working his own land that he was buying after Sophee signed for him. He still lived in his home and continued farming for her.

Sophee began pulling at a buried root of a stubborn vine. She gave it a hard yank, and as it snapped she fell backwards with big lumps of black dirt striking her in the face. Monique screamed, "Are you all right?"

Hoping she had not hurt her baby, she nodded and said, "I am fine, I think."

Sophee was afraid to open her eyes so while in the process of brushing away the dirt by lifting the bottom of her shirt to wipe away the dirt around her eyes, she heard a masculine voice say, "Here, I will help you with that."

Sophee opened her eyes and was surprised to see Koa. She spoke very calmly, "Hello Koa. Welcome back. Your kind services are definitely appreciated."

Koa removed the dirt from around her eyes but considered her face too far gone for temporary repairs. Monique smiled and acknowledged his greetings as she began pushing Martin's carriage to get out of the area of their reunion. Koa congratulated her and told her she had a precious child. Sophee stood while he was admiring Martin. She looked at him. He was thinner and still deeply tanned. She walked toward them as Koa turned, "I would like to shake your hand but I will wait. Since Monique and I are dirty, we will push Martin over to the bird houses so you can see my new project. In addition to everything else at Tillers, I have a Turkey Industry. You will hear them before you see them."

He looked at her as if she were a stranger, "Why do you delight in playing in the dirt? Can't you find laborers for what you are doing? Why do you keep the small child in the sun and dust?"

Sophee noticed criticism in his voice and replied, "A job worth doing is one worth doing yourself. Monique and I know what's blooming when they bloom. That gives us pleasure as well as something worthwhile to do with our time."

"You could find out by reading on the seed packet what's planted."

Sophee was becoming disgusted with his arrogant manner, "Thank you Mr. Superintendent. We have really missed his nagging, haven't we Monique. I wonder how on earth we have come this far without him."

Monique said, "We should have waited for his return."

Sophee laughed and said, "We have been lost without you."

He held up his hand in a truce. "I still think it is unnecessary to labor when there are people who need to earn money, even by playing in the mud."

Sophee and Monique didn't comment since they realized he wanted the last word. When they reached the first house, they found Doug was free to entertain him so Sophee quickly said, "While Doug is free, I'll run over and shower and change. Come on over when you are through here. Thank you Doug, keep him busy for at least thirty minutes."

Doug sensed the tension as he responded, "I'll put him to work shovelling straw. I am certain that would please him and properly initiate him."

Sophee laughed, "I don't think Mr. Declah likes to get dirty but good luck."

She and Monique, pushing Martin, walked over to the cabin and Monique left hurriedly as she requested, "Will you please tell me all that he tells you as excuses for staying away so long?"

Sophee smiled, "I'll give you an accurate report. I can't wait to hear them but I'll fill you and Malcolm in on what he says. Bye, and get that small child out of the sun."

Monique laughed and loaded Martin and his carriage in her truck and left.

Sophee wanted to put on her pants but they didn't meet in the middle. She wore her old black silk shirtwaist which concealed her condition. Wearing her silk scarf as a belt dressed up the severe black. She was waiting when Koa arrived.

He took a long look at her and said, "I see you didn't pine over my absence since you have put on a few pounds."

"A girl has to eat and I stay so terribly busy, I eat more than I should. I have missed you. What kept you?"

"Could we talk over something cool to drink?"

"Iced tea?"

"Yes, a nice tall glass. I had almost forgotten how hot it gets here. You still like living alone in your cabin?"

"Yes, but I have frequent guests. Claire and her family, Emily and Netta visit often and Malcolm and Monique bring Martin, their son, over lots of times and my turkey farmer, Doug and Wally Mehon and their children. All like to visit and fish in the stream. My cousins Jeremiah and Latrelle and their son Jason visit me now since I finally took over the operation of my estate."

"There is still no man in your life?"

"No Koa. I don't take time to look for one. Have you found someone?"

He looked away and when his eyes met hers, he replied, "I fell for you Sophee and wanted you but I did not want your children and I sensed if you married, you would want children since you had failed once as a mother. I felt we were too unstable to bring children into the world. I knew that when we decided to run, the children would be forgotten. I thought about getting surgically fixed and not telling you just so we could be together but I am too honest to cheat, so I stayed away until I got over you enough that I could survive a day without the memory of you torturing me. I am now looking for someone since loving you gave me great pleasure. I must choose a lady who does not want to have children. I came back to explain and to ask you to forgive me for acting like the coward I am. Can you forgive me?"

"Wouldn't a letter or phone call have served your purpose? I forgive you for being a perfect cad. I am happy to report I have completely forgotten any good feeling I held for you."

"No letter or phone calls would have been sufficient. I had to see you. I am glad I came. I feel that you really don't need a man to complement you. You are totally self-sufficient. I don't think now that you would run from responsibility but I also realize I have stayed away too long. I didn't think you would change so much."

"Koa, nothing you say even attempts to mend the gap. It hurts to think you did not want my children. I am glad you made the decision not to return sooner and to forget because I would have wanted you and our children. I think I can be a good mother but you will never know that. Will you?"

"No, and I feel relieved since you may transmit your mental instability to your offspring and after having three healthy, normal children, a sick or deformed child would destroy me. I know I have made best decision for me and perhaps for you."

Sophee stood and without saying a word until she took the picture of his house plan from her living room wall and forcing down her tears and the temptation to crown him with the painting, she extended the frame to him. She breathed deeply and in a voice that quivered with anger, she said, "Koa, take this and leave. Never return to my home again because if you do I can assure you my sanity would be doubted because I would attempt to hurt you physically as you have hurt me emotionally and mentally. If you returned just to punish me and inflict mental cruelty to let me suffer some of your agony, then go, because you dealt the lowest blow I have ever received and it was quite unnecessary. I have been declared sane and mentally sound and have no manner of passing any mental deficiency to my children. Now, get out of my home and my life before I decide to get physical with you."

He held his painting, looked puzzled but took a deep breath and exited her back door, again saying nothing at the last departure. He left as she had ordered him to do.

Before serious crying set in, Sophee called Monique to tell her what Koa wanted. Monique never asked any questions as she quietly stated, "He is not the man I met so many years ago. How do you feel?"

"Glad he came back so I can stop looking for him. Hate him for inferring I suffer mentally and sorry he is an old friend of yours and Malcolm's. I can go on from here as I had planned without him. I am glad I finally felt love so for me there is hope that I can find love that's lasting. I am going for a long ride in the car. I'll see you when I am strong enough to overcome the blow he dealt me."

"Call, if you need anything."

"Thanks Monique. Keep Malcolm away until I can explain to him."

"It will be difficult but I shall try. It is good that this is a very busy time for him. Bye."

"Bye and thanks."

Searching for mental stability that had been severely damaged by Koa's admission of wanting her but not wanting her child, Sophee was sitting on the banks of the stream near her cabin hoping the warm sunshine would inspire her to reach a decision that would bring her peace or despair of having any anticipated future liaison with Koa, the hermit, or with any other male whom she dared love.

She had always vaguely remembered suffering and depending on sunshine as her sole source of comfort and inertia to live since hers had been destroyed rendering her dysfunctional without control from which she had fought very hard to escape and return to reality where she would be free of chasm of doom. She felt too vulnerable to ask anyone why so she survived daily while yearning to delve more deeply into her sub-conscious and bring forth an answer instead of running away from the many spider webs of fear and frustration.

So many times she had felt she was close to finding solution only to fail in her efforts. There was a barrier her delving could not penetrate. She felt a void and loss of continuity like her memory was jumping rope. She wanted to rejoin the skipping links to render her mind to its capability of running smoothly on one even surface rather than on fragile uneven sections. Sunshine consoled her and sedated her, yet she felt it had imprisoned her in a particular time frame that held her against her will and one part was wanting to go back and one part wanting to get out. A certain voice had commanded her conscious mind to return only to leave her suffering and confused sub-conscious mind behind without knowing how to rejoin the two. She felt torn between two realms of reality and feared she would return to the chasm where she had left a vital part of her personality. She rationalized, "I am losing my mind. I must get help. I don't have time to devote to getting my two minds functioning on an even keel. Damn Koa. I am as fit as any woman to have healthy normal babies. Hans is proof of that. No one must know. The people here have either forgotten about my time in the asylum or either have accepted my cure. I wish I had someone to share this dilemma besides You. I'll write down my feelings and let them surface. As I suffer through them alone the second time, then I can be free. I can't lose all that I have accomplished. I am near the brink of survival. It hurts to remember but I shall recall everything and I will survive. Richard, if you weren't already dead, I would gladly kill you now. You took three years of my life. I lived in hell but I never wanted to die. I'll beat this and I'll be whole again. God, give me strength. I prefer living a normal life. Oh God! Hold me in one piece until I can pull the pieces back together. I remember everything. Oh God! I need help."

Poor Sophee wrote and cried, but never called for human help. When her writing and crying episode ended, she read what she had written and accepted it as part of her past. She would carry the precious newness of awareness around with her for awhile but her worst fear was over. She had remembered and relived her trauma alone and was capable of functioning again without stumbling over gaps. She would never marry just to marry, but she would have her own babies. She had the money, a healthy body and an improving mind—so she could find the doctor who had granted her reprieve from her chasm of not knowing and not feeling. She needed to talk and share her findings.

She silently saluted Koa for triggering the sub-conscious to come forth and be healed. She visited the cemetery and assured them their legacy would be kept in proper style. She cried as she released her burden to them and her final cry was the cleansing agent that connected the missing links. "Goodbye Uncle Abram. I truly loved you and I know it is late but I thank you for your love. I will be back very often now. The barrier is gone. It feels like a heavy weight has been lifted. I appreciate the faith you had in me. I hope all of you are listening. Bye dear Uncle Abram. I thank you for my life."

As Sophee watched the last charred piece of her written confession burn to ashes, she sighed. If she could stay hidden until her puffy and very red eyes returned to normal and all evidence of nightmarish tears had dissipated, she would be spared any explanation. When she grew stronger, she would call Dr. Travis Zanuck and let him close her case.

While sitting on the banks of the stream and feeling the healing warmth of the sun, Sophee accepted her frightening realization of having reunited all the existing parts of her being. The why had broken through. It pleased her to know she was not insane and had never been. She had been a victim. Poor misguided and confused Richard. She had been a victim and he had also been a victim. She remembered the incomprehensible pain when Rick took her. She remembered being at the treatment centers. She remembered the horrible fact that she was aware but could not reveal her awareness. She was dwelling in a bottomless pit of unsurmounting darkness. She recalled the good and the harsh treatment. Again she endured the inhumane lack of attention and tender loving care. Her fondest memories were of the soothing voices of Emily, uncle Abram and Dr. Zanuck. She hurt as she realized she had brought him pain and felt mortified with guilt that she had never loved him. Her actions had caused both to suffer needlessly. She had needed him to bridge the muddy waters between sanity and insanity, to extend a steering gear to help her return and to handle ambivalent feeling of leaving or staying and accepting an alive state of an existence of mere vegetation. She knew she would contact him to add her last page in her case history and close the book. If only she could have contacted him in her greatest time of need, however, her applied therapy worked and she was back among the living, although exhausted and hurting. She dared not publish her inability to cope or she would be fired from her seat on the board of Tillers Memorial Medical Center which gave her pleasure and deserved prestige because of who she was and what she represented to many and to honor her dead parents.

Her self revelations were interrupted by a lonely stray mutt, a canine creature which could be positively identified as an apparent hungry and lost dog. He was running along the beach and seeing her, he stopped. He pulled his ears back flat against his head, held his stance like a pointer at a downed bird and then released one ear at a time, first one up and pointed erect and then the other and with both ears up, he looked at her. Then he flopped one ear like folding it and looked at her. Then evidently to gain her interest, he flopped both ears and then with one flopped ear and one pointed ear, he sat on his hind legs and looked at her, just staring. His band of white hair around his neck resembled a clerical collar.

His right front leg looked as though it were encased in a plaster cast including his paw. His short tan hair looked healthy and shiny. His intelligent and charming face had shades of dark and light hair that inspired interest and character of breeding. His brown eyes seemed to be working as a barometer or stethoscope to read and interpret who or what she was and what her intentions were toward him. She had been reduced to a blob of humanity, void of natural functions and feelings and in seeing another, although a mere dog, she identified with him and smiled. They were two straying survivors who needed each other. They each hungered for food, love and protection. She held out her hand to him and said, "Hello pal. I guess you and I have been tossed together by life and perhaps we need to continue the journey the rest of the way together."

She clapped her hands together and said, "Come here boy, come on, you can trust me. Come to me and I'll go inside the house and find food for both of us."

He stood on all four feet and flopped his ears several times and then walked slowly toward her with his long tail tucked close to his body. When she stood, he stopped. She laughed at him and then hearing her healthy laughter, he sauntered toward her, pointed his ears and wagged his tail. He rubbed against her legs and as she reached down to pet him, he pulled his ears back flat against his head and watched her. She spoke, "Easy boy. I see you have survived some suffering of your own. If you hang around here for a little love, room and board, you must have a name. How about 'Memry'? I like it. Let's go home boy. I have to report that I didn't waste myself, but let's eat first."

"Memry'" barked and ran beside Sophee. The sun felt good and she appreciated her former dependence on it. She rejoiced and felt free.

Sophee laughed as she looked down at the dog, "Hey, 'Memry', maybe I should call you 'Why.' You entered my life after I recalled the answers to my many why's. I like 'Memry', since no one will wonder at that name."

Upon completion of their needed baths, Sophee fed them. She called Dr. Traveckie for an appointment to learn if she had damaged her baby during her days of struggle. She did not recall having eaten. She called Claire and touched base with her. She was not alarmed and asked no pertinent questions so she knew nothing of what had happened to her.

Monique assured her the turkey and cattle businesses were thriving and Doug and Malcolm had everything under control. She advised Monique that she would see Malcolm at his home as soon as possible. Strange, Malcolm was only person who needed to know what had happened to her.

That night after Memry had curled up on his blanket at the foot of her bed, she called the Zanuck Clinic to get the doctor's number in case it had changed. When she identified herself, he asked, "Have you met both of you? Is that the purpose of this call?"

It felt as though they had never been separated as doctor and patient as she responded, "Yes, how did you know?"

He chuckled slightly, "As my patient, you never recalled why you were being treated, only that you were. How did it happen?"

"Someone, for whom I cared, said in an insulting and derogatory manner that I was not properly wired. He suggested that I never have any children because of my insanity. My mind snapped back to the time my tortured brain had snapped in the beginning."

"Who helped you through it? I am certain the ordeal was excruciating. You should have called me or some other professional."

"I could not dare involve anyone with my maladjustment. I have a hospital and sit on its board as owner. I dare not be toppled. I would probably snap again if that happened, for sure."

"You sound as if you are now functioning as one happy and sane lady."

She laughed, "I am both. How have you been?"

There was a pause and then he said, "My marriage is on the verge of ending. My wife has been with her family for a long while. I guess I married for wrong reasons, which no longer exist. Have you remarried?"

She laughed, "No, I couldn't face marriage and what it involves before now but through artificial insemination I am pregnant and getting excellent prenatal care and no signs of troubled mind nor body. For the child's sake, I am excited to know I will not be a threat to his genetic disorder. That takes a great burden of fear away from my many concerns."

"Sophee, I will be happy to enter last page of your recorded history at the clinic which by the way is very successful. Not all cases have happy endings but your case is now closed. I would like to visit your hospital and have lunch with you one Monday."

She hesitated briefly and said, "Call when you are free. I can get away any time. I am owner of productive turkey farm here in Longbranch. Perhaps my farm would interest you as much as my hospital."

"You interest me. Talking with you is helping me face my hostilities which have rendered me impotent. Instead of relying on physician heal thyself, I should rely on 'patient heal thy physician.' We have many things to discuss and I am looking forward to seeing you again. You always inspired me to lean on you. Of course you were not aware of that since you leaned on me. I'll call you soon if you give me your number."

"Good. I'm strong enough to see you now. I feel happy, completely happy for the first time in years. Thanks again."

Being alone no longer handicapped her. She had "Memry" to smother with love that no one else wanted, to caress, and to talk to and feel totally in charge of her life. "Memry" would never doubt her nor wonder about her capacity to function as the holder of the Tillers legacy and the mother of her child since her pregnancy was no secret. She proudly began wearing maternity clothes and board members accepted her as they had from the beginning of the hospital's operation. Sophee was not anticipating any cruel gossip about her pregnancy. Her application and approval to become a single mother was carried in all the news media. Folks had been watching for early signs of her planned children. She prayed, "Thank you Lord for restoring my memory and giving me my friend, "Memry." I shall continue to abide in you."

Greater recognition was extended to her as she and Dr. Travis Zanuck toured the hospital. She wanted him to see pediatrics since his success had been with treatment and cure of disturbed children. Dr. Gunter was impressed with Dr. Zanuck and vice versa, so a conference was arranged to negotiate with clinic for consultation and diagnosis of unresponding cases of children in pediatrics.

The good doctor was being taken to lunch at Monique's who had promised to have country feast for Sophee's friend. He relaxed and laughed as ordinary man among friends. He was impressed with Malcolm's knowledge and success in farming and of Sophee's needs. The antics of the turkeys fascinated him and he was quite thorough in investigating the farm's operation. No one gave him any special treatment so he relaxed and enjoyed being a farmer for the day. He was impressed with her cabin but she did not invite him to return to Longbranch. It was his duty to ask to return. She could be close to him and he was no more than Mr. Tom Turkey to her. She wondered if he were conducting his own experiment to determine her state of sanity.

As he stood beside his car before leaving, he turned to her, "Now that I have seen you, I shall overcome my hostile feeling I have held for you since our failed attempt at sex. My wife hopefully will give our marriage a second chance since I can be her active husband. Could we visit sometime? For some strange reason I would like for you to know each other and then my cure would be guaranteed."

103

She almost shouted, "You blame me for your condition?"

He was quick to assure her, "No. No. I don't blame you. You destroyed my ego when I failed to please you so through the years I have suffered. Now that you are in control of your life, I feel that your mental stability helps me to restore my sexual stability. No one else knows of my condition nor why my wife left me without divorcing me. I feel there is hope for total cure for me which will cause my wife to return to me. I would like children but I want to be the father and my wife to be the mother. I have been very lonely and always wanted to call you. Goodbye and thank you."

"Drop in anytime. You are always welcome if you bring your wife. To feel any condition beyond a normally good approach to meeting the long days is an excuse for not having any feelings at all. I can feel now. It isn't sex I care about but honest feelings of all the senses like enjoying daily happenings between sunrise and sunset. I am finally content to just live. My child will give me great pleasure and I can return that to him as I have never been able to before. I have always suffered with inability to stay in one place for a long period of time. Now I feel I can pick any place and stay put for the duration. I fooled myself into thinking that escape was my answer to learn to feel but when I faced my problem, I effected a cure. I feel I have been to hell and back and promise never to return."

He smiled at her and reached out for her hand and held it, "It restores my self confidence and my inflated ego that I was instrumental in part of your treatment which eventually opened the doors to your complete return. I rejoice in your future being free of doubt and escape. Thanks for today. Be happy. You deserve it." He kissed her on the cheek and left.

Visiting Claire at a time when she was at home alone was only time Sophee dared to visit. She wanted her best friend to know she would never run again. She didn't want to paint the picture as it was. She only wanted to let her know she had faced her problem, fought the battles and won. She could finally be a mother to Hans but it was too late to disrupt his secure life. Claire was a very good mother as well as a good person. She and her sheep farm were accepted and many residents had made mutton a large portion of their diet, of course they had their turkey and beef.

She knocked and entered. Claire was going over the books but explained it was time for a break. Over coffee Sophee said, "Claire, I have scratched my final itch. My return from hell is final and I shall never run again. Koa returned and suggested marriage upon condition that he be sterilized since he did not want my crazy children. My poor brain snapped back to reason it originally snapped. I spent seven hellacious days remembering and fighting for total return to sane reality. I won. I feel terribly exhausted. My baby is fine. Dr. Traveckie said I could jump off the tractor and not do it any harm but I don't believe that. He says the embryo is stuck and safe and will stay inside, grow, develop and come out when it is his time. I wanted you to know but I didn't want you to observe the suffering. I yelled, cried and cursed. I called my former psychiatrict and he says there is no need for any treatment. He was happy for me and for him, that he opened the correct door and kept the hinges oiled with his applied therapy that continued through the years."

Claire wiped her tears but more kept falling, "That's the best news you could have given me. Hans has often expressed fear and dread that he might have inherited that trait. I will tell him that external events created the tendency and that you are free of tendency and he should never fear and to enjoy you now in your freedom of choice. You can feel the pangs of motherhood that you missed with Hans. It is not too late to spoil him. He is your child so let him see the normal traits of his mother. He will be impressed and happy to have you at last. I am happy and look forward to being Godmother. Are you through with Koa?"

She laughed, "He is through with me. I owe him. Through his fear of fathering my abnormal children, he triggered the button that realty pushed for the real Sophee to emerge. He has as many problems as I had. We were two basket cases but now I would like to help him but he wants nothing to do with me. He was very explicit at final visit. His burst of indignation cut me free. I am happy for me and sad for him but that won't interfere with my sanity."

When Asa was born, Sophee became a true woman. She loved her son and he made her feel complete. Dr. Traveckie agreed for her second pregnancy when Asa became fourteen months. It worked again and Basil was also healthy and she loved her sons completely. She prayed for the third planned child to be a girl. All the people who were around her laughed at her total devotion. Asa was thirty-seven months and Basil twenty-three months when Dr. Traveckie agreed to attempt her last insemination since three was desired number of children she had chosen even if she had plenty of money and many capable and caring people to help her take care of them.

At the end of her fiscal year, Sophee was relaxed and jubilant over her alarming profits earned from her farming and investments. During the busy months she had filled her turkey houses and the outside pens. She was shipping constantly and she was rushed to supply the demand. She pulled dead birds off the floors without grimacing. She mucked through straw and droppings with ease. She had explained the working operation of the incubator to Claire's and Wally's children so many times she knew exactly how it worked. After telling them it provided constant and adequate warmth and ventilation being electrically heated to maintain constant temperature and how fans circulated the warm air through the egg chamber and over the eggs and that relative humidity was kept at a certain percentage to reduce the loss of water content from the eggs. Their eyes grew large when she explained how the mechanical devices turned the eggs several times daily, turning all eggs at the same time. She puffed as she explained how air that was brought into the incubator kept the oxygen level of outside air. They giggled, "Does it matter if the air is fowl?" She laughed and continued that it took about twenty-eight days for turkeys to hatch and they were amazed at how many eggs could be loaded into the incubator. They wanted to touch the birds when they were taken to the houses and her instructions were finally understood when several spoke almost in unison. "The hens carry out the same process of hatching by sitting on their eggs." They laughed, "Haven't you seen an old setting hen turn her eggs with her beak? How simple? Someone got rich copying nature. I think I'll become an inventor."

CHAPTER SEVENTEEN

Sophee enjoyed her versatile role and enjoyed dressing to assume the role of Ms. Business. With escaping ringlets and sometimes braided and even sometimes in a sedate bun, she reported for work. Going into the office that she was renting from Jeremiah inspired her to dress the part of whatever she could be called. With extra activities at her farm, Sophee had hired a retired teacher to run the office. She enjoyed hearing human voices so she always kept someone near. She worked two full days a week in the office and kept up with it all—with her secretary, Georganne Whitaker, doing the daily postings. She and Doug never could talk over loud gobbles. He worked constantly and managed the laborers he had hired as the business rapidly grew. When to plant was biggest gamble but she followed Doug's and Malcolm's advice and did as they suggested. She kept excellent references.

Her place resembled a boarding school when the children urged their parents to take them to hear the turkeys because they gobbled at sound of car horns. To pacify her birds she blocked off the access road that ran beside their enclosure. Her cattle raising was the least time consuming if she stayed on top of emergencies daily. Her profits remained above average. Her children would be guaranteed a secure future. Basil and Asa were at home around the birds but she felt safer with them at the cabin.

Fearing age might have triggered excessive weight gain which curtailed amount of work energy and simple movement, Sophee simply respected her limited ability and blamed her condition on scheduling her three babies too close, thus damaging her muscles and making her seem so overly large. She delegated. She had hired a general contractor to build her house after she chose the design. She needed more space. Working up until a few days before due dates with Asa and Basil had been easy and free of restrictions. She was becoming anxious but relied heavily on Dr. Traveckie. She went about getting her house. To test the water of credit, she borrowed money to build and did not disturb her available cash or capital. Her profits from her turkeys and cattle had been satisfactory so to keep her expenses in her name, she had her home financed, enjoying the proceeds of her hard work.

Thinking of Claire and her children who were her frequent overnight guests, she chose to have six bedrooms and three bathrooms. Asa and Basil had slept in one section of her bedroom in their separate cribs since they were born and it was almost like having twins since they were so close in age, twenty three months. Orry from Tillers Estate drove over every morning at six and left at six. Sophee took care of them at night and week ends. Jeremiah and Latrelle loved to take them home with them and Jason and Sarah were constant visitors who enjoyed doing things for the boys.

She decided to leave her cabin undisturbed as place of retreat. The boys would have their own private bedroom and the last baby would have Sophee's bedroom to herself. She planned to buy everything new for her home in the clearing. The contractor had planned the perfect location of the house and added extra touches that made it more appropriate for the site and promised her a semicircular driveway and all her necessary buildings which included a horse barn and corral, built as close as possible to the house with the mounting block for the children to get into saddle. Sophee planned to ride and teach her children how and do all the things with them that she had not been able to do with Hans who still did not understand her, yet he assured her he loved her. The contractor painstakingly landscaped the yard to coordinate with the gardens that had been so beautifully restored. Now that Zeus would have companions, she would keep him near. She would have her own riders so she was watching the market for her best horses for the children who resembled her and Hans since the experts in charge of insemination program studied their features and interrogated Sophee about her family coloring and genetic build. They teased her, "You will have children who will resemble you so select the father to match them to guarantee coordination of family color and design."

Dr. Traveckie cautioned Sophee to be prepared for early delivery on her last visit to see him. He gave no reason other than birth was imminent although early. Upon arriving home, she and Orry packed her suitcase and included her spare cosmetic kit that contained her personal items. Sophee chose a white going home outfit for the baby. She wanted a girl so she planned to play it safe by choosing neutral. The suitcase was put into the car which had a full tank of gas. All the necessary phone numbers were beside the phone. Orry's was most important since she had to sit with the boys, the doctor's so he would be waiting for her to arrive at the hospital and Claire's to drive her to the hospital. She figured the third time would be routine so Sophee felt confident in relying on her friends. Her family was abroad on a long vacation. She had been pre-admitted so all she had to do was show up at the hospital, a long ride from her home. Returning home from her weekly visit to the doctor, Sophee was very surprised to find her crew and friends had moved her.

One Saturday morning, way before daylight and three weeks before due date, Sophee had been awakened by labor pains which she recognized as real. Rain was coming down in torrents which frightened her. Her doctor had been only one to answer her call. When she realized she had to take her children with her, aroused Asa and Basil and carried them to the car after trying to reach Malcolm one last time. She covered the boys with blankets and drove herself to the hospital. She made it but pains were very close and her fear didn't add to her discomfort. She had laughed as she tossed Basil's diaper bag in the backseat since as with Asa and Basil, she would have two babies in diapers but only one on the bottle since Basil had been weaned. She would be happy in new house,

Later Sophee drove into the emergency entrance where her boys were removed from the car and taken to the lobby as a nurse rolled her to the labor room and carried her luggage. She learned later two kind nurses had taken the boys in and placed them on the couch in the lobby and covered them with their familiar blankets. They asked the admissions clerk to keep an eye on them. Asa at forty-seven months and Basil at twenty four months would probably cry when they awoke since they were too young to feel secure in a strange place without her but she was still doing the best she could. She had used her only alternative after her well-laid plans were altered, hopefully by logical explanation and not deliberate act of making plans for another activity. They planned their lives around her due date, not the one that was so very early. Celie and Delie Tillers, perfectly formed twin girls arrived less than an hour after Sophee arrived at the hospital. Celie weighed five pounds and two ounces and Delie weighed five pounds. There were lots of activity and many calls for extra doctors to report to labor room, "Stat" shortly after Sophee had returned to her private room. She called Claire who promised to come immediately. Sophee slept until Claire arrived. Asa and Basil had been cared for by a strange man who had brought in a lady in labor. Sophee's call to her could not get through because the line had been knocked out by a limb on the line and it had been restored only minutes before Sophee's morning call from the hospital. Claire touched Sophee's arm as she stood quietly by her bed. Sophee smiled as she saw her friend and asked, "Have you seen them?"

Claire smiled, "Yes. Both of them. They are adorable. Did you know you were carrying twins?"

Sophee smiled, "I only knew I was much larger with them. Dr Traveckie says he didn't hear two heartbeats. We were both surprised."

"How long were you in labor?"

"I was here for only about an hour but I knew I was cutting it close by trying to reach you, Orry and Malcolm. I am glad it's over. I prayed very hard to get here. I could hardly see and the contractions were very fierce. I didn't make it alone. He watched over me. Are the boys still sleeping?"

"No. Schwinn is with them. Some man was with them when we arrived. They were not afraid but he looks beat."

"There was some kind of emergency in the delivery room shortly after I was rolled out of recovery. Have you heard what happened?"

"No, but don't you worry. We'll go now. I know the boys are hungry. I'll keep them until I can get Orry. I know little Basil needs a diaper change. I saw his bag. I'll change him before we leave.

If you don't object, we just might keep them for the full time you will be in the hospital. It is always nice to have babies at our house. Hans takes excellent care of Asa and Basil, of course he has always been the best sitter for Tabitha. I love you. I'm sorry about not being there for you. Take care."

Sophee held on to her hand and said, "Keep them if you like but please let Orry know. Thank you and Schwinn. Tell the boys I love them and I love you and Schwinn, too. Please bring another white outfit for the other baby to wear home and bring blankets. Bye now. My children need you."

Looking frumpy and fat but feeling lighter in her black robe, Sophee ambled down long corridor to the nursery. Her babies were sleeping so she looked for features that were not hers. She thought about the sperm donor and wandered if he could recognize his offspring. She would never know the father of any of her babies, but she knew the expense of what they had cost, but they were worth much more. Even so, she loved them and would be free of a father's influence. After giving thanks for her healthy babies as assured by Dr. Traveckie, Tharpe would take over their care as he did for Asa and Basil who loved him. She walked over to look at the tiny baby in one of the incubators. It looked like a doll except for its arms and legs that were moving rapidly. Sophee smiled at the determined baby. She sensed another person beside her. She turned her head to ask if he were the father when she realized he was crying as he watched the baby. Sophee asked, "The baby will be all right, won't it?"

He never tried to hide his tears as he spoke, "No one guarantees anything at this point for her or her mother. She is two and one half months premature and only weighs three pounds."

Sophee asked, "What happened to the mother?"

"Her blood pressure went too high and created danger for her and the baby. The mother is hooked up to enough gadgets to get her through this with His help."

Sophee wanted to hold him as she replied, "I hope they both make it. The baby seems determined in spite of all odds to stay alive."

He looked at her as if he was seeing her for the first time. "Thank you. Which one is yours?"

Sophee smiled at him as she answered, "Both of the Tillers' baby girls are mine."

He crushed her to him and cried unashamedly. He kept his face buried in her robe and cried. She stood until he composed himself.

He released her and said, "Thank you. I needed to hold onto someone. I feel totally helpless and alone. I hope I don't offend you since you have just delivered twins."

Sophee asked, "How is your wife?"

He looked confused as he explained, "The baby's mama is not my wife. She is my twin sister. There has been no change since she was admitted."

"Was there a condition that caused the elevated blood pressure?"

"I can't call it that since she did it all the time. Her husband is in service and when he left for another assignment on short notice, they decided she could drive down here to be with me when the baby came rather than remain alone. She did that with her second son with no trouble. She has two boys five and three who are at my neighbor's house. She began gushing blood but with no pain about five miles out of town. She explained immediately and I removed the boys from the car and ran with them to my neighbor's house and asked her to alert the hospital that a threatened miscarriage was coming in."

"You must be the strange man who kept my two boys entertained until my friend arrived?"

"Yes, the small one cried but I changed his diaper and sang him to sleep. When the older one saw the younger one was safe, he too fell asleep. Where is their father?"

Sophee smiled, "Might still be at the bank."

"You are teasing me, I hope."

"Yes, I guess. Are you married?"

"Not any more. I was married for fifteen years to a wonderful woman who refused to have my children. When I finally succeeded in getting on as a professor of history at Loo's College here in Stratford, she refused to leave her comfortable way of life and come with me. Shortly after my arrival here, we agreed to a quiet uncontested divorce. My sister, Eva, very pregnant and the mother of Eric, age two, drove across country with the rest of my things I could not pack in my car. We had fun in getting my one bedroom apartment livable. I am Dr. Epps Hollander, but call me Epps, please."

Sophee smiled, "Hello Epps. I am Sophee Tillers, farmer and former nurse. I live in Longbranch but my doctor is Dr. Traveckie who owns this hospital."

"Since you have two babies, can I claim one for my own? I would be happy. I choose Celie since she wins by two ounces over Delie. I'll be there to spoil her after Eva and Maria pull through. Will you say a special prayer for them?"

"This is not the day they gave babies away. If you would like to visit Delie and Celie, I guess you can be there to spoil all of us. It's time for the doctor to make his rounds. I'll see you."

"Give directions to your farm before you leave."

She laughed at his excitement, "Just ask for turkey farm. Anyone can tell you how to get there. I promise to say a prayer for them."

The next day when Sophee visited the nursery, a large gathering of adults stood near the tiny baby. They greeted her as they joined her. The father, Major Trepp Ranew, had been flown to be with his family. He said, "You are Sophee, the turkey farmer and mother of twin girls and two boys and a friend of Epps?"

She received his brisk hug as he introduced his parents, Timothy and Patrice Ranew and Epps' parents, Mose and Anise Hollander. Mrs. Hollander said, "Thank you for being so kind to Epps. He didn't panic because you were here, he told us. It was terrible for him since he and Eva are so close. She is hanging on to life by a thin thread and the baby is improving. We are bringing the boys, Eric and Griff, in to see their mother and pray their voices reach through to her.

The doctors are trying everything they have here at the hospital and she has been placed on several prayer lists."

Sophee asked, "Are they still at Epps' neighbors?"

"Yes, she and the other neighbors have been very kind. Since Epps only has one bedroom, Mr. Hollander and I are staying at his neighbor's where the boys are."

Sophee asked, "Is there anything I can do other than have a dressed turkey delivered this afternoon? Give me the name and address so I can call and have it delivered."

"You are really a turkey farmer? I thought it was a joke. Send it to Epps apartment, here it is. Thank you. We shall enjoy it. May we visit the farm?"

"Be my guests, anytime. I hope Eva and her baby pull through. I'll say a prayer for them. My mother died shortly after my birth. I understand how vital it is that she live!"

Epps' mother let the tears flow as she replied, "Bless you. Thank you for giving Epps support although you probably didn't realize what you were doing."

"He must be a very nice person. He changed my son's diaper and we had never met. I was forced to bring them with me and leave them in the lobby under the care of the admission clerk until my friend arrived. He entertained them and I was told he sang Basil to sleep while Asa grinned at him since they liked him evidently but Asa watched him closely. I guess we helped each other. Glad to have met you Mrs. Hollander. I must return to meet the doctor."

"We will see you at the farm. I promise."

On the afternoon that Claire and Monique brought the children to see the new babies, Sophee was excited. They stood and admired them. Trepp was with his wife but the Hollanders and Ranews met them and showed them tiny Maria. They wanted to get a closer look since they had never seen such a tiny baby. Epps came while they were gathered near the nursery. Sophee introduced him to Claire and Monique and Asa and Basil smiled at him since they remembered him. Epps held Tabitha, Basil, Asa and Martin so they could get a better view of the babies. He remembered all their names and told them goodbye by saying each name and not forgetting a single one. Sophee said, "Well done. I would never try that in public."

Epps laughed, "I get better."

Sophee visited briefly for the five days of her confinement and on the last day, the family had been assured Eva and the baby were out of danger but Eva was still unconscious. Epps hugged her in front of the family, "When I get a chance, I am coming to see you and the children, my two boys and my two girls. Get ready to be spoiled. I hope they are as hungry for spoiling, pampering and nurturing as I am. I am a man of my word so beware."

She smiled and said, "I hope your conditioning is only temporary. You sound confused. However, I am very glad that Eva is improving."

"Thank you. I'll be seeing you." He kissed her on her cheek and smiled, and walked away.

Setting up a workable routine with twins brought forth all of Sophee's prior experience and knowledge of handling enthusiastic friends. There was a parade of people who loved her so she let the callers come inside and allowed all who wanted to see Celie, Delie and her new house which she had yet to enjoy. They cooed at the babies to get smiles for their pictures and Asa and Basil laughed at them because after hearing them cry several nights, it was great to hear the adults talk baby talk. The extra space in her new home made it easier for Sophee. She could keep Asa and Basil contented in their cozy bedroom and keep Memry safely locked in her bedroom since he didn't like the parade of visitors and had begun barking at everyone. He seemed to jump for joy when everyone left and he had Sophee to himself.

It took about three weeks for all the concerned friends to pay them a visit. Emily became a permanent guest and hired Scotsia to help Orry while she supervised the running of the household and especially caring for Sophee whom she considered her daughter. Sophee resumed her work since Emily was in charge. She began working her two days at the office of Tillers Estate and checked on Doug's and Malcolm's bookkeeping and was thrilled to find she had not been missed because everything was in order. To show gratitude and respect to her people on the land, Sophee asked Malcolm to plan an "Open House" celebration to last as long as they wanted with food and games and lots of talking. Malcolm and Monique had their own celebration. Monique delivered twin boys, Archer and Lance. She was not surprised since twins were due in her generation. Sophee laughed as she realized she had inherited that trait for her girls. Malcolm and Monique's large families volunteered to help and Malcolm threatened to leave home because of the noisy household, but he was a proud father as he cautioned Monique, "Be prepared to have a big family if you plan to have two for one since I will have one daughter."

Monique said, "You are the boss?"

He smiled, "About this, I am. Give me a daughter."

Everyone laughed because Monique also wanted a daughter.

CHAPTER EIGHTEEN

Epps kept his word. He brought Eric and Grif who soon felt at home and didn't want to leave. He brought his parents who chose to go fishing and he brought Trepp and his parents who loved her garden. He always brought Asa and Basil something. They rolled on the floor with him. He had dinner with them. He and Jeremiah, Latrelle, Jason and Sarah had become friends. Claire and Schwinn liked him and the children treated him like a celebrity since he was a college professor. Memry loved him and was more partial to him than Sophee when Epps was in the home. Malcolm and Monique loved him and admired the expert manner in which he treated their horses. Doug and Wally were always happy to see him since he always pitched in and helped with whatever they were doing. Hans never gave him any special attention.

He loved to walk in the garden and was happy to learn how Sophee felt about being welcomed there by the former owners. If Epps arrived home before Sophee returned to the house, he helped Emily with dinner and watched the preparation of bottles, bath and bedtime. He was like an uncle to them since they depended on him for love. She often wondered if his students were suffering since he spent so many evenings with them.

It was a thrilling moment the day he brought Eva, Maria, Eric and Grif. He carried Maria and walked beside Eva. Sophee seemed to be seeing him for the first time. Her heart pounded and she knew she would faint. She couldn't take her eyes off him. She had known him for many weeks and had always enjoyed being with him. She wasn't prepared to accept that she was in love. She hoped to keep it from him. He was very good with the children who loved him. What a mess!

Epps stopped near her, leaned over and kissed her on the cheek and said, "This visit is very special. It is a chance for you to meet two great fighters. Eva Ranew, meet Sophee Tillers. The doctors have dismissed both patients and promise both a complete recovery. This is Maria's first outing. She now weighs five pounds and one ounce. They are leaving me to join Trepp who is coming for them. He doesn't want Eva to drive yet so he is flying in and driving them back to their home on the base. He will drive Eva's car. We want you to have dinner with us tomorrow night at the "Cattle Drive", a fancy restaurant in Stratford. Think about it. Be there at seven in formal dress. It is a special occasion. Will you go?"

She was barely able to invite them in but no one apparently noticed any change in her. Malcolm dropped by to remind her of the cattle auction at which she wanted to sell her steers that were ready for market and buy new feeders. Sophee introduced him to Epps, since he had never been at home while Epps rode his horses, "Mr. Petrie, Dr. Hollander, Malcolm, Epps."

Each gave the other a complete once over and while they were making up their minds about each other, she introduced him to Eva, Maria, Eric and Grif. Malcolm asked, "Are you the one who changed Basil's diaper at the hospital?"

Epps looked rather shocked as he replied, "Yes, but that's all I did. He needed changing badly."

Malcolm laughed and placed his hand on his shoulder, "Don't apologize. I want to thank you for helping her out. Everyone she needed that night was away on business or couldn't be reached. It hurt me to know she needed me and Monique. We were at the hospital here in Longbranch spending the night with a sick friend. Thank you. I appreciate what you did. Any man who would do that for my friend is a friend of mine. Mrs. Eva you have a very fine brother who also knows horses and takes good care of them. Welcome to Longbranch. I believe she said you are a college professor who is at Loo's University. Monique, my wife, completed her undergraduate work there and she applies her knowledge as my wife and our children's mother. Come over anytime. Our home is yours to enjoy. You may continue riding the horses and can begin feeding the cattle. One thing that is not on my land is a turkey so to laugh at them you know where you have to go. You have a fine little girl. I have twin boys and my wife has promised to give me a girl one day. Our oldest son, Martin, is proud of his brothers."

Epps was smiling, "I am glad to know Sophee has good friends like you and your wife. The next time I am here, I'll drop by and after feeding your stock, I'll enjoy a long ride. Thank you. I appreciate what you are doing for me as Sophee's friend. I have been told how you feel about turkeys."

Malcolm was in a hurry as usual as he spoke, "I must hurry. I have a few more chores to finish before calling it a day." He shook Epps' hand and patted Eva on the shoulder and hugged Sophee and then left.

After coffee and cake and an interesting visit, Epps and his sister began gathering the children. Emily carried Maria and walked along with Eva. Epps held Sophee's arm as he spoke, "Tomorrow at seven. "Cattle Drive" is three blocks north of the hospital. You can't miss it. The parking area has security patrols so feel safe to park and walk inside. Will you be there? It is very important to me."

He had beautiful hazel eyes which were warm and pleading—daring her to say no as she replied, "I'll be there and dressed in the formal style you requested. Why is it important?"

He laughed at her, kissed her on the cheek and said, "Don't ask. Please be there."

Eric and Grif from the back seat of Epps' car yelled, "Thought we were leaving!"

Epps signalled to them that he was leaving as Sophee laughed and said, "All right. I'll wait and find out why tomorrow night."

He kissed her on the cheek again and saw that Eva and Maria were in the front seat. He opened the car door and eased in, smiled and drove away. Her heart was still pounding and her knees were weak. She rushed back inside and petted Memry, then sat down to wait for Emily. She began to dream and felt confident that she could accept her love for Epps if he could love her. She whispered to Memry, "Old boy, you are the first to know how I feel, but I think I'm in love." She kissed him and he snuggled closer to her.

Emily, Orry and Scotsia smiled but never questioned Sophee when she announced she was going shopping next morning. She went directly to "Formals by Ken" since she always found her size there. She couldn't get into either of her two formals but being plump never phased her—given time she would return to her normal weight. Epps had seen her looking frumpy without any makeup and liked her enough to ask her out so she would attempt to create glamour with what she had to work with while achieving the desired look.

When the sales clerk brought out two dresses, she immediately chose the mauve silk crepe that concealed her plumpness. When she arrived home for the big show, she was relieved that her boys and Emily, Orry and Scotsia liked the dress. They succeeded in putting her hair up. The long tendrils that refused to stay, they let dangle close to her face. Her diamond necklace and earrings completed her formal look and she was pleased. She wore her black evening jacket and her black silk pumps and purse. She was nervous and was afraid she would create a catastrophe. She felt it was the first real date of her life. Once she was in the car after kissing her children and repeating instructions about where she would be. She had always left Asa and Basil with Claire, Monique or Wally but Tabatha, Martin and Yevette had chicken pox so she was leaving all four children and Memry at home.

She parked and prayed as she walked that she would not make any mistakes to scare Epps. She had decided to let her feelings run wild and if it was love she was feeling she was anticipating great pleasure and enjoyment. She recalled Epps' statement that his wife had refused to have his kids and rationalized she had four children at home and Hans.

She would be willing to give him at least two and prayed he would accept her home as his since she felt she could never leave after learning how to stay.

Without the added ingredient necessitated by imminent birth, the ride to the "Cattle Drive" had seemed shorter. The parking lot was filled with luxury cars. Sophee was not intimidated since her attire was luxuriously appropriate, her hair was stylish and her luxury car was current model. She was happy with her final accomplishment even though it had been too long since she had dressed to go out. Her present life was preferred, her children and work made her very comfortable and kept her busy. Her lifestyle had been segmented and was not one of continuity. She knew she would only reveal answers to Epps' questions. She was the prize and not the surprise. Every outing was to fast food establishments to buy food that could be held in their hands by passing table etiquette. In becoming a mother she had changed her preferences and lived for her children and work, each very rewarding. She had resorted to childish whims since it was convenient not to have to dress all of them for a fancy outing. They would grow and on that she hoped to survive her detour.

Koa had taken the wind out of her sails but Epps had silently crept in without making demands on her but in pampering her children and getting to know her and accept her friends and family. Tonight she was debuting as the woman who would share her future with a man if Epps asked her. He had not asked any questions of her but she knew he must know she was a single mother or he would not have become a constant visitor at her home and he definitely would not be seen in public with her. She wondered how much he knew. After scaring off Koa, she would provide all answers very carefully and not volunteer any facts. He was pursuing her and so far quite honorably. She would not analyze any overt actions. She was having fun and decided to walk into any situation with Epps by taking one slow step at a time. Every one around her had someone to share their love. She had her children and Memry and after meeting Epps she wanted more—that what others had.

She had finally won the acceptance of the townspeople when she settled on the estate and forced its residents to attend the farm meetings and take part in what concerned them and by bringing another industry to Longbranch. Hard work had mellowed her and shaded her desire to run. She regretted losing the love and companionship of her first born but there were some things that could not be corrected. Her new confidence had kept Hans as a good friend but not as her son. She had accepted her mistakes and had chartered another route to dare to succeed as a mother which gave her great happiness and worth.

When Sophee entered the lobby of the restaurant, she realized she had accepted an invitation to a royal banquet, much more than formal. An employee in white tie and tails greeted her, "Are you Mrs. Tillers?"

She smiled at him and said, "Yes, but how did you know? I am not wearing a nameplate. Did Dr. Hollander ask you to meet me here in the lobby?"

He smiled and said, "Yes. This is his night and he is being congratulated by so many that he was afraid he would be detained and miss you when you arrived. He asked me since I am one of his students who happens to be working my way through college by working here."

She was becoming excited as she asked, "Why is he being honored?"

"For his outstanding work in the state competition among the students interested in history. The Governor asked him to organize the program. No one knew that he would take the chance and involve all the school and all the media. He is being given the Olaf Otto Humanitarian award for his efforts."

She was surprised and shocked as she exclaimed, "Why would he invite me to share in such a prestigious affair?"

117

He smiled at her, "Mrs. Tillers, I guess you are the last to know you are his chosen lady. He is very proud of you. There is a seat at the head table for you between him and his mother. His sister, father and brother-in-law and his family are here. He is so excited that probably someone will have to tell him what happened here tonight. Governor Sprague is the presenter and the first lady is with him."

"Now I know why he insisted on my dressing formally. I should have been more persistent in asking why I was told to come in formal attire, I am here so I must see what's in store for me. Do you escort me to him?"

"Yes. Here is the corsage he asked me to give you and help you with it in any way if you needed my services."

She laughed as she accepted the corsage, "What a man! I am certain his students enjoy being in his classes."

He was beaming, "Yes we do. You look great. Ready for me to escort you to him?"

She looked up at him and smiled, "I would like to leave my butterflies here in the lobby. I'm ready. Thank you very much."

Someone had been thoughtful in keeping the lights down low as she walked slowly up to the table where Epps stood and smiled without moving. They looked at each other in stark wonder. Finally she was near as he reached out both hands to her. "Thank you Wendell for taking care of Mrs. Tillers. You may go now. I see you both did an excellent job with the corsage."

The young man bowed and left. He was beaming. Epps asked, "How did you succeed in being the most glamorous lady here and the most beautiful?"

She smiled, "I merely dressed as you requested or rather ordered. The dress is new but everything else has been around for awhile."

He held her hand as he said very softly, "Thank you for coming. Did Wendell fill you in on what this occasion is all about?"

"Yes, but you could have prepared me. Congratulations. Wendell is very impressed with what you did and so am I. Why didn't you explain?"

"I couldn't. I sounded like an egostical oaf in telling Eva, Trepp and my folks. I wanted you to share this with me. I didn't want to turn you away."

"I would have come. It is an honor to be here. Thank you."

Sophee greeted his family again and after the dinner and speeches and award, she met Governor and Mrs. Sprague who requested Epps' presence at a private meeting in the Governor's suite. He had not been informed so he simply shrugged, kissed Sophee on the cheek and said, "I'll call you when this is over. Are you going home now?"

She felt uncomfortable as she replied, "I would love to be seen in this expensive gown longer than two hours but I don't wish to go out alone nor to go with your family. Don't call. It will be too late. I am thrilled that you invited me tonight. I'll see you around."

As she began walking away, he stood near the Governor and his team. He seemed confused. She smiled and he relaxed.

Taking inventory had always been her top priority. She began her tangent. She preferred her life as it was with Asa, Basil, Celie and Delie. Her friends were very dear to her and her surrogate mother, Emily, was there to care for her. An evening at home after the children were asleep meant reading and relaxing to good music with Memry at her feet. Being alone and undisturbed could be tolerated, with nothing being required of her.

Epps apparently was ambitious and happy in the lime light as center of attention. His family worshipped him and he reciprocated that love. She felt she could never give up her independence, her home, and her legacy and heritage and move away. For the first time in her life she felt she belonged. She was really accepted and recognized. Jason constantly reminded her that she had become more successful in the stock market than he had been. Her quarterly gatherings had become an exciting and an unbelievable event. Doug and Wally and family, Malcolm, Monique and family, and Claire, Schwinn and family were her dearest and closest friends. Her tenants reverred her and she had no more space to give to others.

Tharpe had finally accepted her as more than "big boss lady" after she chose him as the children's pediatrician. To get away to breathe Sophee spent quality time at her cabin just being there with Memry. No one disturbed her. They thought her running to the cabin was better for everyone and her, so they took care of her babies and her responsibilities. She thought she would never run again. She prayed for an answer to find her reason for getting away, far away, yet she loved what she was doing. Others accepted what life offered but Sophee became driven by some inner power to leave and find peace. She wore her yoke well and it fit too loosely. Only Memry heard her crying.

Being unable to sleep, Sophee slipped her black satin robe over her matching pajamas and after checking on the four sleeping babies, Emily, and Scotsia who had chosen to spend the night, she pulled out a good book and headed for the kitchen to brew some coffee.

She sensed disaster when the rapid pounding began at the front door. She yelled, "Who is it?"

A familiar voice replied, "Epps. I must see you. Please let me in."

Sophee opened the door and before she could ask him to come in, he pulled her into his arms and held her to him for a long time and then gently eased her from him, "Don't ever leave me as you did tonight. I was paralyzed with fear that something had gone wrong. I apologize for not knowing the Governor wanted a private conference but you could have waited with my family which you stated that was not what you wanted. What happened?"

She looked at him and answered, "I felt I was interferring where I had no business being there."

"I wanted you beside me. You are my business. Traveckie and I completed our undergraduate work together. He went into medicine and I went into education. He admires you for daring to be different and not involving any other living soul you chose to have your family by using your money instead of your love."

"He was unethical. He had no right to betray my confidence. I had no choice, I had the money but I did not have the love. I used what I had."

He looked frightened as he explained, "He didn't betray you. I saw your chart and when I spoke of you, he told me without revealing your name."

"Whatever? It hurts that he told you."

He kept his distance as he continued, "Sophee, I love you and your children. That's all that matters to me. My love for you and hopefully your love for me. Certainly we have lived as we so desired up until now. That made us what we are which entertained love and respect but now I would like to begin life again with you. Will you marry me? I know you can't leave your holdings and responsibilities here. May I live here with you? My apartment is too small for all of us."

She was happy but surprised as she spoke, "Epps, you are very strange to even dare to assume the responsibility of four small children and a wife who would not be an asset to your future. You are too ambitious and I am too nondescript and rural."

He leaned out to hold her, "I only want to teach until I retire, nothing more. If possible, I'd like for you to have my children. I want to share my life with you. I wish I had met you sooner so we could have more time together."

"You accept me as I am?"

"For better or for worse. I fell in love with you when you stood in your robe and gown looking at your babies. You were perfect specimen of woman. I knew you had to be mine."

She smiled, "I fell in love with you the day you brought Maria from the hospital. I must warn you. I will test your love but I'll marry you and you may share my home and the work and all the headaches of what being a Tillers involve."

"I want all of you."

"I surrender gladly."

They shared their first kiss. Both were shocked at the passion between them. Epps held her hand and walked her to the door, leaned over, kissed her very timidly, smiled and said, "Becoming a Hollander won't be any easier on you. They will demand an elaborate wedding for all relatives to attend so they can see whom I have chosen. They love hard and are loyal and dedicated to everlasting happiness, love and family life, especially children. I will tell them after we have had time to make our own plans and I give you your engagement ring."

"Did you rush over here just to propose marriage?"

He smiled at her, "No. I thought you did not want any part of my life. I was scared when you walked away. I could not have lived another minute without seeing you and finding out how you felt. The timing is lousy but I am happy to know we are getting married. Let's marry first and meet friends and families later."

"That suits me. It's late so you must be going. We will make our wedding plans the next time we meet. Goodnight."

"Say it again."

"I love you, Epps Hollander."

"I love you Sophee Tillers."

He left too soon, Celie and Delie awoke for their bottle and changes. She laughed as she imagined their fulfillment among four children and two who cried for what they wanted. She took Celie while Scotsia took Delie thus cutting the feeding time in half and allowing Emily to get her sleep. Sophee cuddled both of them and kissed them goodnight. She felt they were spoiled since at their ages, babies usually slept through the night. She gave them her undivided attention and enjoyed loving all four of them at their chosen hour to have her to themselves without sharing her with the other three.

Sophee placed her book on the nightstand since she could not force herself to read. She was too excited to read or sleep and in the early hours of morning she dared not call Malcolm, Claire, nor Jason to tell them her good news. She confided in Memry and hugged him.

Her family and friends were finally getting what they wanted for her. She reached to turn out the light just as the phone rang. She dreaded calls in the night which represented an emergency. Hesitantly she answered and heard Epps' voice, "I called to say I love you."

She asked, "Wherever did you learn how to make a woman happy?"

"Somewhere along the way by learning through my mistakes. I kept the things that worked, stored them in my mind and only use them when I am certain it is the right woman. This is the first time I have had a chance to try them out."

She smiled, "I am thankful that you have me on whom to apply your love strategies. Life with you is going to be one excitement after another. I look forward to having them work."

"Not as much as I do. I now feel almost complete. The trail ends with us together, to enjoy or discard what we have learned along the way. Goodnight love."

"Goodnight Epps."

As she replaced the receiver, she said, "Goodbye loneliness."